S0-BNW-925

THE WONDERS OF OUR WORLD

Forests

Neil Morris

CRABTREE PUBLISHING COMPANY

www.crabtreebooks.com

The Wonders of our World

Crabtree Publishing Company

Author: Neil Morris
Managing editor: Jackie Fortey
Editors: Penny Clarke & Greg Nickles
Designer: Richard Rowan
Production manager: Chris Legee
Picture research: Robert Francis

Picture Credits:
Artists: Martin Camm 11, 13, 20; Cecilia Fitzsimons 8, 17 (bottom); Chris Forsey 27; John Hutchinson 4; Deborah Johnson 17, 29; Paul Williams 11, 13, 18
Maps: AND Map Graphics Ltd.
Photographs: Canadian Pacific Railway 11; Robert Francis cover, 3, 4, 5, 9 (bottom) 14 (top), 15 (right), 17, 18, 19 (top), 23 (top left), 25 (bottom), 26 (bottom), 26-27, 28 (bottom), 29; Robert Harding Picture Library 7, 9 (top), 17 (bottom), 20-21, 22 (bottom right), 23 (bottom); Hutchinson Picture Library 10, 12 (bottom), 14 (bottom), 15 (top and bottom left), 16 (bottom), 22 (top), 23 (top right), 24, 24-25, 27, 28 (top); Caroline Jones 6; Sue Rose-Smith 25 (top); Science Photo Library 20;
All other photographs by Digital Stock and Digital Vision.

Crabtree Publishing Company
www.crabtreebooks.com 1-800-387-7650

 In Canada: We acknowledge the financial support of the Government of Canada through the Book Publishing Industry Development Program (BPIDP) for our publishing activities.

Cataloging-in-publication data

Morris, Neil
Forests / Neil Morris
p. cm. — (The Wonders of our world)
Includes index.
ISBN 0-86505-833-4 (library bound) ISBN 0-86505-845-8 (pbk).
Summary: Text and photographs examine various aspects of these natural wonders including their formations, wildlife, and histories.
1. Forests and forestry—Juvenile literature. 2. Forest ecology—Juvenile literature. [1. Forests and forestry. 2. Forest ecology. 3. Ecology.] I. Title. II. Series: Morris, Neil. Wonders of our world.

QH86.M67 1998 j557.3 LC 98-107766 CIP

Published in the United States
PMB 16A
350 Fifth Ave.
Suite 3308
New York, NY
10118

Published in Canada
616 Welland Ave.,
St. Catharines,
Ontario, Canada
L2M 5V6

Published in the United Kingdom
73 Lime Walk
Headington
Oxford
0X3 7AD
United Kingdom

Published in Australia
386 Mt. Alexander Rd.,
Ascot Vale (Melbourne)
V1C 3032

CONTENTS

WHAT IS A FOREST?

A FOREST is a large area of land that is thickly covered with trees. Smaller, less dense forests are called woods or woodlands.

Different types of forests grow in different climates and at different altitudes. The tropical rainforests for example, found in hot, rainy places near the equator, are different than the conifer forests of the world's cooler or more mountainous regions.

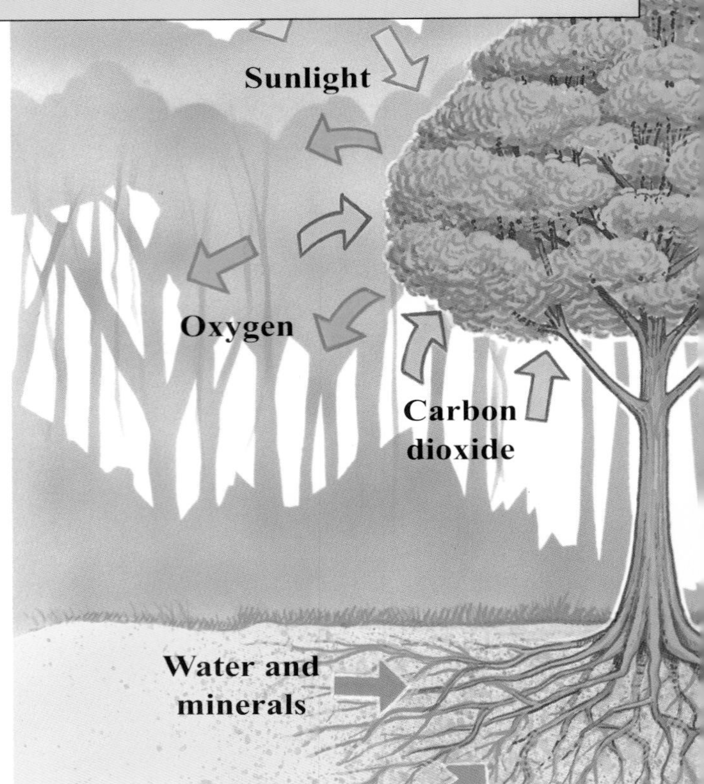

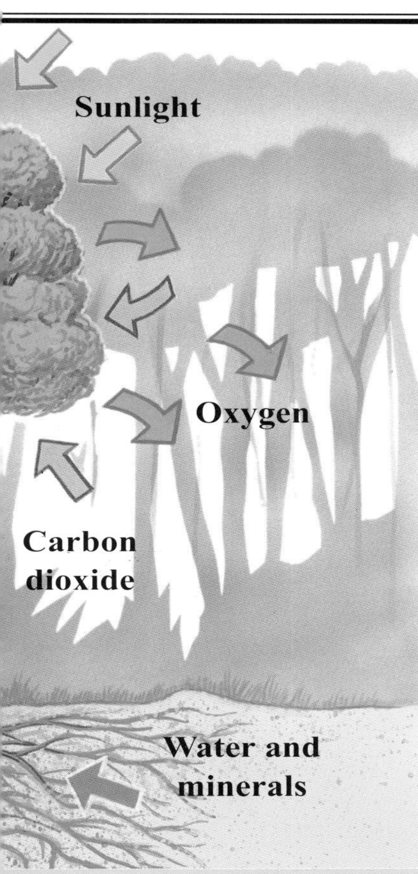

FOOD FOR TREES

Like all plants, the trees in a forest use sunlight to make their food (left). Chlorophyll, the green substance in their leaves, captures the energy in sunlight. Trees also take in carbon dioxide, a gas in the air, and mix it with water and minerals from the soil. During this process, trees give out the oxygen that animals and people need to breathe.

RAINFOREST MONKEYS

Forests are home to countless animals, such as capuchins (above). Capuchins live in the tropical forests of Central America, and spend most of their time high in the trees.

PLANT LIFE

Ferns and other small plants often cover the floor of a forest, such as the one in New Zealand shown left. In this cool, wet region, mosses and other plants grow on the trunks of the tall trees. All of these forest plants soak up a lot of rain. They stop the water from wearing away the soil and help prevent flooding.

CLEARING THE LAND

For thousands of years, people have been cutting down trees for timber. They have also cleared the land to make way for farms and towns. Now people are concerned, because vast areas of the world's forests are being destroyed.

WHERE IN THE WORLD?

FORESTS COVER more than a quarter of the earth's land area. They are found all over the world, except near the poles in the Arctic and Antarctic, and in deserts. In the polar regions, it is too cold for trees to grow, and in deserts, too dry.

Boreal forests stretch across northern Europe, Asia, and North America, where winters are harsh and summers are short. Temperate forests grow in mild regions, where there are warm summers and cool winters. Tropical forests are found near the equator, in the hottest part of the world.

THE WORLD'S FORESTS
Different kinds of forests grow in bands across the world (left).

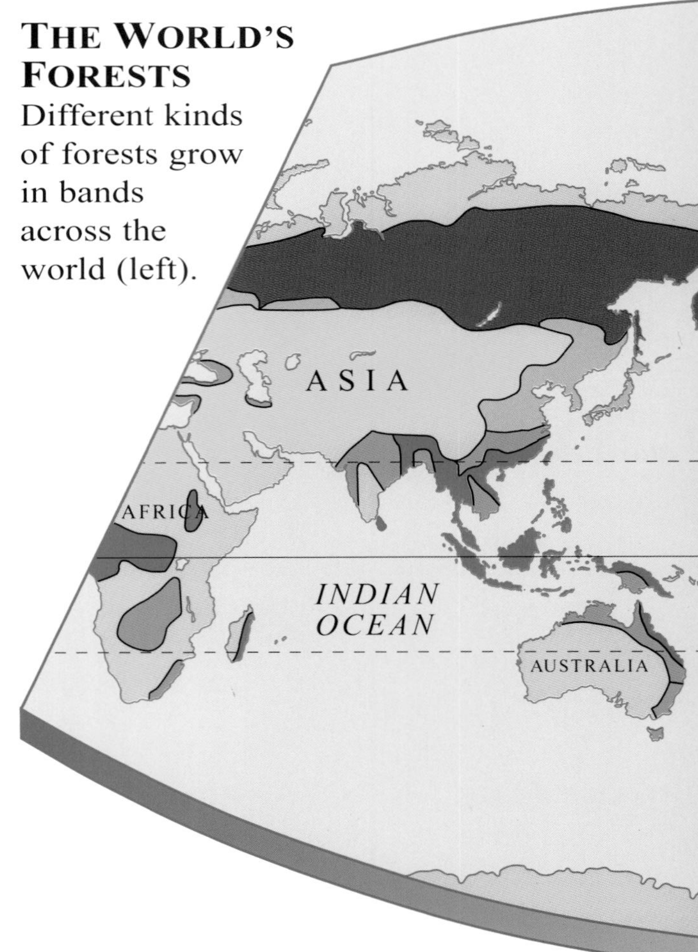

GUM TREES
Eucalyptus trees once grew only in Australian forests, such as the one shown left. Then people planted these tall, fast-growing trees in California, southern Europe, and other warm regions. Eucalyptus leaves contain gum and a valuable oil that is used in medicine.

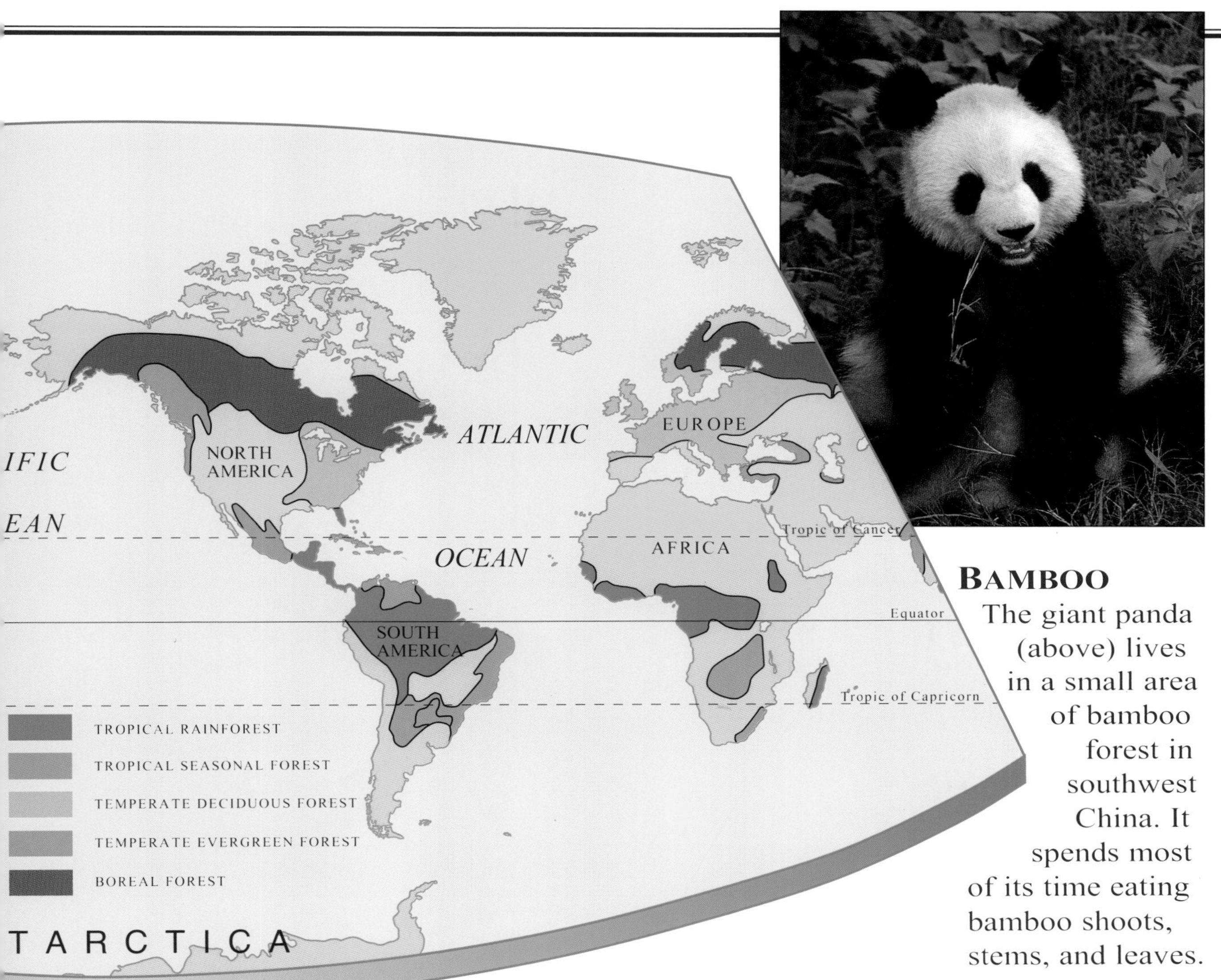

BAMBOO

The giant panda (above) lives in a small area of bamboo forest in southwest China. It spends most of its time eating bamboo shoots, stems, and leaves.

MEDITERRANEAN HILLS

IN areas with hot summers and mild winters, such as the lands around the Mediterranean Sea (right), tough, low bushes grow in place of tall trees. This hilly scrubland is in the southern part of Spain.

How Forests Grew

THE FIRST forests grew on marshy land hundreds of millions of years ago, when trees were like giant ferns. As the land dried out, new trees with needle-like leaves appeared. Over millions of years, the earth's climate changed, and forests of broad-leaf trees developed. In the Ice Ages, glaciers destroyed some of these forests, but the trees grew again when the ice melted.

JURASSIC FORESTS
Dinosaurs (right) appeared 230 million years ago, and lived in the forests for 165 million years.

SWAMP FORESTS
About 300 million years ago, the first forests (below) were full of tree ferns, club mosses, and horsetails. Amphibians came out of the water to live on land.

PREHISTORIC TREE TRUNK

THE stone trunk above is about 200 million years old. It is one of thousands in Petrified Forest National Park, in Arizona, USA. In prehistoric times, the forest was buried in volcanic ash, mud, and sand, which formed rocks. Wind and rain slowly wore away the rocks, leaving the tree trunks. These ancient trees were like pine trees.

COAL

IN the early swamp forests, layers of dead plants were buried in mud. Over millions of years, pressure turned the buried material into peat, and then into coal. The layers are easy to see at this open-cast coal mine in Australia (right).

In the North

VAST FORESTS stretch across the northern regions of North America, Europe, and Asia. The long winters mean that these forests are often covered in snow, and the growing season for the trees is very short. Almost all boreal trees are conifers, with tough, needle-like leaves, and bear their seeds in cones. Most are evergreen, which means they keep their leaves year-round.

World's Biggest Forest

The taiga, which is another word for boreal forest, stretches over 6,200 miles (10 000 kilometers) across the whole of northern Russia, from the Baltic Sea in the west to the Pacific Ocean in the east. Some of the world's longest rivers wind their way through the vast forest (below) to the Arctic Sea. North of the taiga is the frozen, treeless Arctic. South of the taiga are the warmer plains and grasslands of the Russian great steppes.

Canada

CANADA'S forests stretch across the country, covering about half its land area. In many places, the forest (right) is broken up by lakes, as well as by the swampy ground called muskeg.

DIFFERENT CONIFERS
The conifers above belong to the pine family. They are evergreens except for larch, which drops its leaves in the fall.

GRIZZLY BEAR

Bears, beavers, moose, wolves, and foxes are among the larger animals of the boreal forest. North American grizzly bears seek out ice-cold rivers (right), where they can catch salmon swimming upstream to breed.

IN MILD ZONES

TEMPERATE FORESTS grow where the climate is mild, such as in parts of North America, Europe, and China. These places have warm summers, cool winters, and plenty of rain year-round.

Many temperate forests are full of deciduous broad-leaf trees, which shed their leaves each fall. The trees do this to save energy and moisture, and spend the winter as if they were asleep. They grow new leaves each spring. Temperate forests on steep slopes are usually made up of evergreen conifers.

REDWOODS

REDWOODS (left) are huge conifers that grow in temperate evergreen forests near the west coast of the USA. Redwoods are the world's tallest trees, and can grow to 328 feet (100 meters) high. These huge trees stop most of the sunlight from reaching the forest floor.

FALL COLORS

As deciduous trees prepare for the winter, the green chlorophyll in their leaves fades. The chemical processes involved cause the trees, such as these in Maine, USA (left), to show the typical fall colors of red, yellow and brown.

BROAD-LEAF TREES

Most broad-leaf trees in temperate forests, such as ash, beech, maple, and oak, are deciduous (above). The leaves of many of them turn brilliant colors in the fall. In warm climates, some oak trees are evergreen.

EVERGREEN FOREST

The evergreen forests of New Zealand are home to rare flightless birds, such as kiwis (right). During the day, kiwis hide in burrows or among tree roots. They come out at night to find food – worms, insects, fruit, and leaves. The kiwi has no tail, and its stumpy wings are hidden in its hairy-looking feathers.

TROPICAL FORESTS

TROPICAL RAINFORESTS grow near the equator on warm, wet lowlands. Of all the world's forests, these have the greatest variety of trees. Most are broad-leaf evergreen trees, and many are up to 130 feet (40 meters) high. The forest's ground is covered by a thick undergrowth that we call jungle.

Other kinds of tropical forests, including some in Africa, India, and China, have both rainy and dry seasons each year.

RARE RHINOCEROS

Southeast Asian rainforests are home to the Sumatran rhino (below), sometimes called the hairy rhinoceros. These animals have been hunted for their horns and are now in danger of becoming extinct.

AMAZON RAINFOREST

THE thick forest around the Amazon River (left), in South America, forms the biggest rainforest in the world. Every day, however, parts of the forest are cut down to make way for farmland and roads (right).

Buttress Roots

MANY of giant rainforest trees have huge buttress roots (above). These jut out from the lower part of the trunk to give the tree a wide base and so help support it.

Plants Growing On Trees

Epiphytes, or air plants, grow on tree branches without harming them. They are common in tropical forests. Epiphytes, such as these bromeliads (below) growing on a eucalyptus tree, have clusters of leaves that hold a lot of water. They sometimes grow in tiny pockets of soil that form in the bark of trees.

MOUNTAINS AND COASTS

IN THE mountains, it gets colder as you go higher. The changing temperatures affect mountain forests. Broad-leaf temperate forests grow on the foothills, but on higher, colder slopes, evergreen conifers grow instead. These conifer forests, such as those in the European Alps and southern parts of the Rockies, are similar to boreal forests.

Along the warm, muddy coasts of many tropical regions, belts of swampy mangrove forest grow. Mangroves are the only trees in the world that can grow in salt water.

TREE LINES

On tall mountains, there is a limit above which trees will not grow because of the cold. This limit is called the tree line, and it can be seen in the Swiss Alps (above). There are conifers up to the line, and a few tough grasses and plants above it. The peak of the Matterhorn, in the background, reaches 14,692 feet (4 478 meters). There is also a tree line in freezing northern regions, such as Siberia (left). North of the line is a cold, treeless zone called the tundra.

Mangrove Roots

Mangroves have prop roots that curve down from their trunk (above). These roots are above the water level, and take in the air the trees need. The trees' main roots grow down into the swampy mud.

Snow Leopard

The snow leopard (below) lives in the high mountains of the Himalayas. When winter comes and the weather turns even colder than usual, the snow leopard moves down to the lower forests. It hunts deer, goats, marmots, and other small animals.

Goshawk

Goshawks (above) are large birds of prey that live in the forests of North America, Europe, and Asia. With a wingspan of 4 feet (1.2 meters), goshawks fly fast among the trees after their prey of hares, squirrels, and birds. In mountain forests where snow lies in winter, goshawks are paler than those living further south.

FOREST LAYERS

TREES ARE not the only plants that grow in forests. Forests are made up of layers of plants. If enough sunlight reaches the forest floor, ferns and flowers grow, forming the herb layer. Taller shrubs, or woody plants, form the next layer up. Above is the understory, a layer of short or young trees. At the very top is the canopy, made by the tops of the tallest trees. It gets the most sunlight, and forms a roof over the other layers.

ON THE FOREST FLOOR
Many mushrooms and other fungi grow on the forest floor. Some, like the glistening ink-caps above, grow on the trunks and stumps of dead or dying trees.

TOWERING UP

THE layers of a temperate deciduous forest are shown left. If the forest has an open canopy, the shrub layer is often thick with bushes. Many of the trees that form the understory will eventually grow to reach the canopy. Many types of birds and animals live in the different forest layers.

RAINFOREST CANOPY

The canopy of a rainforest (above) usually has three layers. The trees of the upper canopy grow to about 130 feet (40 meters). A few may be even taller. The middle canopy usually reaches about 65 feet (20 meters), and the lower canopy about 33 feet (10 meters) above ground. The shrub and herb layers are usually thin because very little sunlight gets through the canopies.

BABY RACCOONS

MOST raccoons live in wooded areas, often in small family groups. They have strong, sharp claws, and spend much of their life climbing in trees. They make dens in hollow logs, stumps, or trees, and come out at night to hunt for their food. They eat nuts, fruit, and small animals, such as frogs and fish.

ANIMALS ON THE GROUND

JUST LIKE trees and plants, the animals that live in a forest vary according to what sort it is. In temperate regions, worms, snails, mites, ants, and beetles all feed on the leaves that fall from the trees. In rainforests, the floor is damp, so animals such as leeches, flatworms, and land crabs are common, as are many different frogs. In all forests, large animals feed on smaller ones, while leaves, fruit, and nuts are food for plant eaters.

FOREST ELEPHANT
African elephants (right) live in the forests and bushland of central and western Africa. Living among trees, elephants eat mainly leaves and fruits, as well as grass and roots. Sometimes they strip bark from a tree with their strong tusks for a quick snack.

ARMY ANTS

IN most forests, ants live on the ground in large groups called colonies. Army ants, such as the one left, are always on the move. They travel in columns through the Amazon rainforest, eating other insects and larger animals.

Elk

ELKS, or wapiti, are big North American deer that eat grass, leaves, and small plants. Males (right) have antlers, but the females do not. In winter, herds of elk move south to find more sheltered forests.

Badgers

The Old World badger (below), found all over Europe and northern Asia, is larger than its American cousin. Badgers use their strong claws to dig long underground burrows, called setts, which they fill with bracken and other vegetation for bedding. They come out at night to feed on small rodents, worms, insects, nuts, and berries.

Biggest Cat

The Siberian tiger (above) lives in the forests of northeastern Asia. The biggest of all the big cats, its body is up to 9 feet (2.8 meters) long, with a tail about 3 feet (90 centimeters) in length. Its thick coat keeps it warm in the bitterly cold winters. Unfortunately, there are few of these cats left.

IN THE TREES

THERE IS a wealth of animal life in a forest's trees. Different kinds of birds live and nest in them – from toucans and macaws in rainforests to woodpeckers and owls in cooler wooded regions.

Some animals live only in certain areas. For example, the orangutan lives only in the rainforest on two Asian islands. The koala lives only in the eucalyptus trees of Australia.

TOUCAN
Different kinds of toucans (above) live in the rainforests of Central and South America. They use their huge bills to pick fruit and berries from tropical trees.

KOALA

ALTHOUGH they are often called koala bears, Australian koalas (left) are not bears. Koalas are marsupials, which means the female carries her young in a pouch. Koalas eat the leaves and shoots of certain eucalyptus trees. They only come down to the ground to move to another eucalyptus tree.

RED SQUIRREL
An American red squirrel grasps a branch with its strong paws (above). Squirrels help the forest by burying nuts. Many of these nuts grow into new trees.

TREE SNAKE

SOME snakes live in trees, using their tails to hang from branches. The eyelash viper (above) of Central America is about 20 inches (50 centimeters) long. It gets its name from the raised scales over its eyes.

ORANGUTAN

Orangutans (above) are the largest tree-dwelling mammals. They eat and sleep in the trees, swinging between branches to move through the rainforest. The orangutan's name means "man of the forest" in the Malay language.

CHIMPANZEE

Chimps live in the rainforests of Africa (right). Like orangutans, they are at home in the trees and sleep in nests made of branches. Chimps, however, spend more time on the ground, searching for food.

PEOPLE OF THE FOREST

THROUGHOUT THE centuries, people have lived in forests without destroying them. The Pygmies of central Africa, for example, have lived by hunting animals and gathering plants. Living in small groups, they move from camp to camp in search of food, building huts as they go.

Pygmies see the forest as the giver of life. It gives them food, clothing, and shelter, so they try not to harm it. Now, however, outsiders are cutting down the forests, destroying the Pygmies' home.

THE KAYAPO
This young Kayapo boy (below, center) holds a ceremonial headdress. The Kayapo live in the Amazon rainforest of Brazil. They grow maize and sweet potatoes in their forest villages. Like many other forest peoples, the Kayapo are losing their traditional land.

PYGMIES
Central African pygmies (below, left) build their huts of saplings and leaves. The Mbuti Pygmies of the Ituri forest are thought to be the shortest people in the world. Some adult women are just 4 feet (1.24 meters) tall.

In the Woodlands

THIS photograph, taken in the early 1900s, shows a Cree settlement in North America. Cree people once lived in the forests and woodlands of eastern Canada. Their tent homes, called tepees, were made of skin or bark stretched over wooden poles. Men hunted and fished, while women and children gathered roots, berries, fruits, and nuts in the forest.

Fruit of the Forest

The Dayak woman below is choosing jackfruit in the market. Many different Dayak groups live on the island of Borneo, in southeast Asia, which is part of Malaysia and part of Indonesia. Some Dayaks still live in their traditional longhouses, with up to 50 families per house.

USING WOOD

WE USE wood every day. In many parts of the world, wood is the main fuel for cooking and heating. It is used everywhere to make furniture and build homes. In factories, paper and plastics are just two of the things made from wood. Humans use up a huge number of trees! In managed forests, new trees are planted to replace those cut down. Replacement is only possible, however, when fast-growing conifers are planted.

WOOD MOUNTAIN
At the plant in Australia shown above, pine logs are cut up into tiny wood chips to be used for making paper or chipboard. The wood chips are piled high next to the plant.

LOGGING
When trees have been felled (right), the logs are taken to a sawmill. Today, this is usually done with cranes, tractors, and forklift trucks. If a river is nearby, the logs are floated to the sawmill.

Recycling Paper

Recycling plants, such as the one in Indonesia shown below, turn paper back into pulp and make it into new paper. The plants serve two purposes — they reduce the number of trees we must cut down to produce the pulp from which paper is made. They also solve the problem of what to do with waste paper.

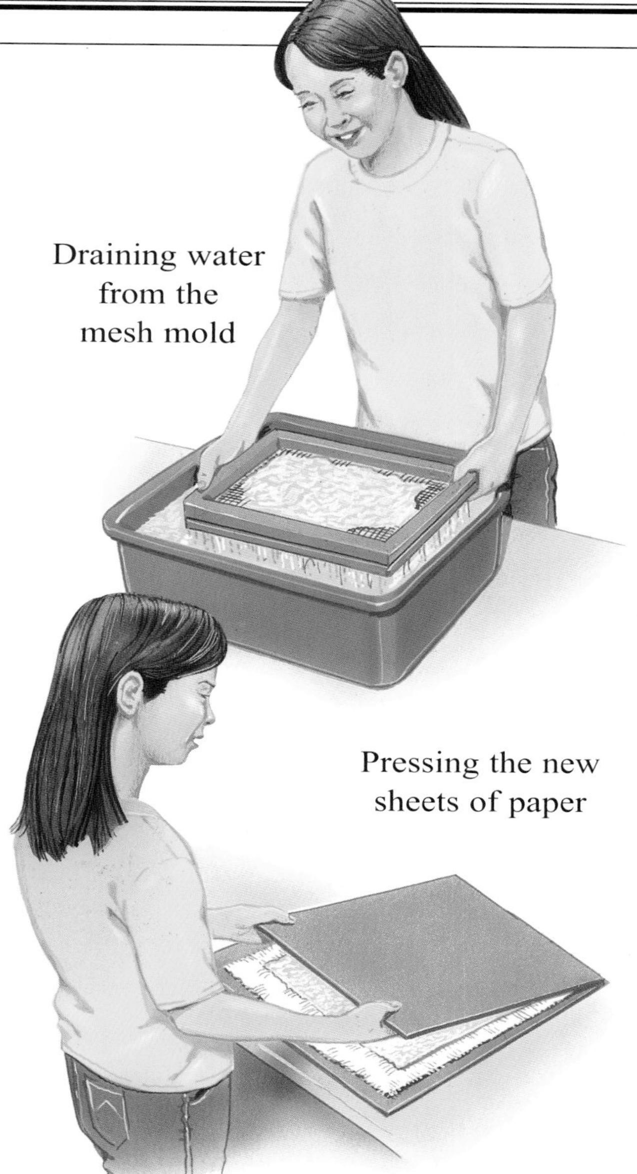

Draining water from the mesh mold

Pressing the new sheets of paper

Making Paper

The Chinese invented paper over 2,000 years ago. They made pulp by mixing the bark of mulberry trees with water. Then they put it on a mesh mold and let it dry. We can still make paper in the same way today (above) as a craft or a hobby, but most paper is now made in large factories.

TODAY AND TOMORROW

MANY FORESTS are in danger. People cut down trees much faster than they plant them. Even when new trees are planted, it takes years for them to grow and replace those that were cut down in only a few minutes.

The clearing of forests is called deforestation. Fortunately, it is slowing down, but 115 square miles (300 square kilometers) of forest are still cut down every day. Rainforests are in the most danger, which means that everything that lives in them is also threatened.

FOREST ON FIRE
The great Amazon rainforest (above) has suffered more than most forests in recent years. Huge areas are burned to clear the land for cattle farming and to make roads to reach the interior of the forest.

SLASH AND BURN

PEOPLE in many countries burn patches of forest to grow their food. In Indonesia (left), big companies have done this, leaving dead forests and a smoky smog.

PLANNING FOR THE FUTURE

THOUGHT and planning are needed to preserve our forests. The scientist above is checking seedlings of different kinds of trees before they are planted in Mount Rainier National Park, USA. In protected areas such as this, visitors can enjoy the forest's natural beauty.

PROTECTING FOREST LIFE

PROTECTED areas can help stop the problems of deforestation. In Poland and Belarus, a national park of ancient spruce forest has been created to save the European bison (below), which was in danger of dying out.

GLOSSARY

Amphibian An animal that lives on land and breeds in water

Bird of prey A bird that hunts animals and other birds for food

Boreal forest A forest of the earth's northern regions, mainly made up of conifers

Broad-leaf tree Any tree with wide, flat leaves instead of needles

Bushland Land that is partly covered with shrubs and some small trees

Canopy The top, leafy layer of trees in a forest

Chipboard A building material made by pressing wood chips together

Chlorophyll A green substance in plants that captures the energy in sunlight and helps to make the plants' food

Conifer A tree with needle-like leaves that bears its seeds in cones. Most conifers are evergreen.

Deciduous Describing trees that shed their leaves in the fall

Deforestation The process of stripping the land of forests and trees

Epiphyte A type of plant that grows on a tree without harming it

Equator An imaginary circle that stretches around the middle of the earth

Evergreen Describing trees that keep their leaves year-round

Extinct Describing a type of animal that has died out

Glacier A slowly moving mass of ice

Ice Age A time when ice sheets covered large areas of the planet

Jungle The thick, tangled undergrowth in a tropical forest

Jurassic	The period, over 140 million years ago, when dinosaurs lived on Earth
Marsupial	A type of mammal. Female marsupials carry their young in a pouch.
Mineral	A natural substance, such as salt, coal, or gold, found in the earth
Muskeg	A Canadian word for flat, swampy ground found in the North
Pulp	A soft, mushy substance made from wood, used in papermaking
Rainforest	A very wet, thick forest found in warm tropical areas
Recycle	To treat or break down waste material, such as glass, paper, or tin, so that it can be used again.
Scrubland	Dry land with tough bushes and short trees
Slash and burn	A method of clearing land for farming by cutting down trees and other plants and setting fire to them
Steppe	A Russian word for a flat grassy plain
Taiga	The huge boreal forest that stretches across northern Russia, between the tundra and the steppes.
Temperate forest	A forest, mainly made up of deciduous trees, found in the mild regions of the world
Tepee	A Native American tent home made of skin or bark
Tree line	The level on a mountain, or in far northern regions, beyond which no trees grow
Tropical	Describing something in the tropics, near the equator
Tundra	A cold, treeless part of the Arctic where the ground is always frozen beneath the surface

INDEX

6 7 8 9 0 Printed in the U.S.A. 7 6 5

Y0-BPT-434

Jennifer A. Lindbeck
Jeffrey B. Snyder
Elegant
Seneca
VICTORIAN
DEPRESSION
MODERN
Schiffer Publishing Ltd
30 Lower Valley Road, Atglen, PA 19310 USA

In memory of Robert Elliot Johnston and to the Johnston family—whose great generosity and love will remain a constant remembrance of mine.
~Jennifer A. Lindbeck

To Mom and Dad—Jim and Mary Alice. Thanks for everything you have done, and continue to do, for me. Your love and guidance have brought me to the path I travel today.
~Jeffrey B. Snyder

Library of Congress Cataloging-in-Publication Data

Lindbeck, Jennifer A.
Elegant Seneca/Jennifer A. Lindbeck, Jeffrey B. Snyder.
p. cm.
ISBN 0-7643-1141-7 (hardcover)
1. Seneca Glass Company--Catalogs. 2. Glassware--United States--History--20th century--Catalogs. I. Snyder, Jeffrey B. II. Title.
NK5198.S39 A4 2001
748.29154'52--dc21
00-010147

Designed by "Sue"
Type set in ZaphChan Bd BT/Aldine721 BT

ISBN: 0-7643-1141-7
Printed in China
1 2 3 4

Published by Schiffer Publishing Ltd.
4880 Lower Valley Road
Atglen, PA 19310
Phone: (610) 593-1777; Fax: (610) 593-2002
E-mail: Schifferbk@aol.com
Please visit our web site catalog at
www.schifferbooks.com
We are always looking for people to write books on new and related subjects. If you have an idea for a book please contact us at the above address.

This book may be purchased from the publisher.
Include $3.95 for shipping.
Please try your bookstore first.
You may write for a free catalog.

In Europe, Schiffer books are distributed by
Bushwood Books
6 Marksbury Ave.
Kew Gardens
Surrey TW9 4JF England
Phone: 44 (0)208 392-8585
Fax: 44 (0)208 392-9876
E-mail: Bushwd@aol.com
Free postage in the UK. Europe: air mail at cost

Acknowledgments

Thanks to the efforts, expertise, willingness, and direction of so many individuals, I present to you this marvelous display of glassware from the Seneca Glass Company:

To collectors Jim & Marjorie Wiley (active members of Old Morgantown Glass Collectors' Guild, P.O. Box 849, Morgantown, WV, 26505) for their initial contact, enthusiasm, valuable time in proofing the captions and pricing the items, and their coordination of the Seneca collections to be photographed.

Also to Jim & Marjorie, collectors Linda & Michael Hall, and Kurt Ly for opening their lovely homes (and Kurt's terrific restaurant) and agreeably allowing their space to serve as a photo studio. Each is to be especially thanked for their exquisite collections of Seneca glassware, which are pictured throughout this book.

To John & Marsha Brand and Pamela Ball Redmond of the Seneca Center (formerly the Seneca Glass factory), and Riverfront Museum, Inc. for opening the Seneca Center and granting photography of the historical displays and murals that cover its inner walls and corridors—I hope that this book may forward your work in preserving the history of the company and original factory.

To Christy Venham and staff of the West Virginia and Regional History Collection, West Virginia Libraries, for unearthing numerous historical documents, articles, and texts about the Seneca Glass Company, its history and wares—your efforts and keen research assistance proved more than worthy for writing the text of this book.

And, finally, *many* thanks to Jeffrey Snyder for stepping up to provide the text and pass along his glassware's expertise and years of experience; Blair Loughrey for his skillful and talented photography, and for the fun times in Morgantown—you will be missed; Robyn Stoltzfus for her efforts and hard work, which are not applauded enough; Becky Riggins for her time spent numbering; and Sue Taltoan for the book design and layout.

Preface

The Seneca Glass Company identified the vast majority of their wares by line numbers (or stem numbers when dealing with stemwares). These numbers allowed the company to positively identify their products to their workers and were essential for internal use, as these numbers were much less ambiguous than the advertising department's descriptive names for products. When available, we have used the line/stem numbers in the captions first (listed as Line or Stem as appropriate) to identify the wares. This information is followed by the description of each piece, its cut or decoration (when available), and any further pertinent information such as measurements. Lastly, prices are included in the captions; however, NP (**n**o **p**rice) occasionally appears when no valuation is available. Wares for which line numbers are unavailable appear first in each section to keep matters organized.

To aid the reader, glassware items are further organized into sections according to ware type (e.g. bowls, pitchers, tumblers). One exception exists (doesn't it always?). Seneca Series items (Cascade, Driftwood Casual, and The Fashionables—late-comers to the product lines) have a section to themselves. All these sections, from ashtrays to vases, are arranged alphabetically for easy use.

We hope you enjoy the book and wish you the best of luck in your search for Seneca glassware.

—Jennifer A. Lindbeck & Jeffrey B. Snyder

Contents

Introduction

In 1891, a group of immigrant glass artisans and businessmen from Germany's Black Forest region settled in Seneca County, Ohio. Seeking to take advantage of the opportunities available in the American glass market, they took possession of the former Fostoria Glass Company factory and established the Seneca Glass Company—so named for the county in which the factory resided and a regional Indian tribe of the same name. Soon opportunity beckoned elsewhere. Attracted by the lure of cheap natural gas, free land, abundant quality glass sand within easy reach, and a city subsidy, the company was moved to Morgantown, West Virginia, in 1896. While the location changed, the Seneca name remained. Over the years, the Seneca Glass Company developed a reputation for creating some of the finest hand-made lead crystal glassware available nationally and worldwide.

Pen & ink of Seneca Glass Co., The Gray Ptg. Co./ Engravers & Printers/ Fostoria, Ohio. *Courtesy of the Seneca Center and Riverfront Museums, Inc.*

Certificate of Incorporation

STATE OF WEST VIRGINIA

I, ——— Secretary of State of the State of West Virginia, hereby certify that an Agreement duly acknowledged and accompanied by the proper affidavits, has been this day delivered to me, which Agreement is in the words and figures following:

Wherefore, The corporators named in the said Agreement and who have signed the same, and their successors and assigns are hereby declared to be from this date until the ——— day of ——— nineteen hundred ——— a Corporation by the name and for the purposes set forth in said Agreement.

Given under my hand and the Great Seal of the said State, at the City of Charleston this ——— day of ——— eighteen hundred and ———

Secretary of State

Seneca Glass Company certificate of Incorporation, circa 1891. *Courtesy of the Seneca Center and Riverfront Museums, Inc.*

Over some ninety-two years of production—the firm would cease operations in 1983, Seneca produced quality, delicate, lead, blown table and barware in a wide variety of forms. Stemware, tumblers, goblets, jugs, water bottles, finger bowls, nappies, and more were all produced in abundance. The company is best known for the striking cut glass patterns they produced. Some of the patterns were so complex, they took an experienced cutter twelve hours to complete. This high quality lead crystal tended to be expensive. Author Martha Manning put it well in her 1984 article "West Virginia Cut Glass": "clearly [Seneca cut glass was] intended only for the tables of the very rich and the very careful." In later years, management would boast of having over one thousand cut glass patterns available to their customers. If you need to replace a twenty-year-old Seneca stem cut in a pattern no longer produced, that was not a problem. Seneca kept an extensive pattern archives!

Grouping of line 903, square base, cut 121 Laurel pattern: iced tea, 6" h. $15-25; water goblet, 6" h. $15-25; champagne, 5" h. $15-25; cocktail, 4" h. $15-25; wine, 4.5" h. $15-25; low wine, 3.75" h. $15-25; bells, 4" h. $25-35 and 3.5" h. $20-30; pitcher, cut 121 Laurel pattern and 39, 6" h. $75-80; plates, 6.5", 8", 8.5" dia. $15-20.

Line 190, cut 641: finger bowl, footed, 4.5" dia. $15-20; finger bowl, 5" dia. $15-20; On the Rocks, 3.5" h. $15-20; tumbler, 4.75" h. $15-20; water goblet, 5.25" h. $20-25; iced tea, 6" h. $20-25; juice, 4.5" h. $20-25; cocktail, 3.5" h. $20-25; whiskey, 2.5" h. $20-25.

Line 475, cut 786 Butterfly pattern: iced tea, 6" h. $20-25, water goblet, 7.5" h. $20-25; wine, 6" h. $20-25; cordial, 4.5" h. $20-25; juice, 4.5" h. $20-25; cocktail, 3.5" h. $20-25; water goblet, footed, 5" h. $20-25; tumblers, one 5" h. and two 3.75" h. $15-20 ea.; finger bowl, 5" h. $15-20.

Wide-ranging offerings in a variety of decorations, colors, and price ranges were vital to the survival of any twentieth-century American glass firm. The Seneca Glass Company also produced wares decorated with needle and plate etchings and sandblasted decorations. Other decorative techniques were also available, including banding and metallic decorations. Unlike the irascible Henry Ford, who proclaimed you could have his car in any color you liked so long as it was black, Seneca did not eschew color in favor of their beautiful clear crystal. While lead crystal would be what consumers thought of first when they thought of Seneca glass, the company did offer a variety of colored glasswares from around the 1920s onward. The quantities of colorful glasses and tablewares available fluctuated over the decades with the ever-changing public taste. Colored glassware would be offered in larger amounts during the later decades of production, beginning around the 1950s. Later colorful glassware lines included Brocado, Cascade, Driftwood Casual, The Fashionables, and Quilt.

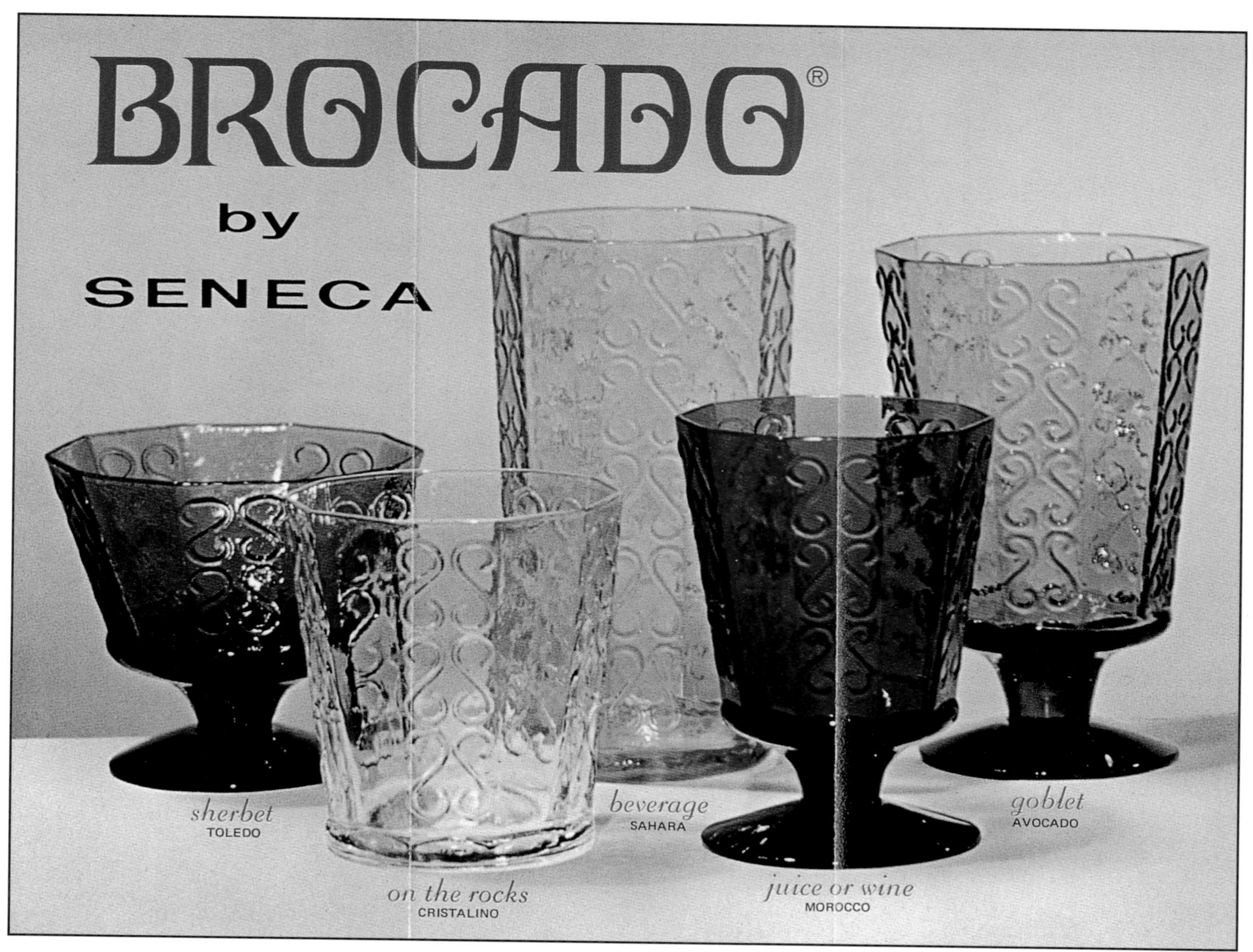

"The excitement of the Mediterranean is BROCADO, the handblown, fire-tempered glassware by Seneca. Each of the five distinctive shapes is your invitation to entertain . . . to add a fresh, informal elegance to your table, patio or bar. You can be hostess to a happening with BROCADO." From company brochure, no date.

The Fashionables. From *Catalogue No. 72*, pg. 3.

"Durable enough for everyday, handsome enough for entertaining . . . that's handblown, fire-polished Driftwood Casual by Seneca! The jewel-like colors are crafted into the glass, to never scratch, peel, wear or fade." From company brochure, no date.

From *Catalogue No. 77*, pg. 14.

The Seneca Glass Company enjoyed the patronage of many notable and famous businesses and individuals. Over the years, Seneca received orders for their glassware from the Ritz Carlton Hotel in Boston, the Sheraton Palace Hotel in San Francisco, Marshall Fields and Company in Chicago, B. Altman's and Tiffany's in New York, and Neiman-Marcas in Dallas. Philadelphia's highly regarded John Wanamaker department store, known for its pipe organ and massive eagle sculpture, placed an order for 218 dozen glassware items, all cut with the crest of the President of Liberia and destined for his executive mansion. (Page 1995, x)

Tumbler, etched and cut for Hotel Astor, 5.5" h. $10-15.

Wine glass, manufactured for the Aladdin Hotel, in Las Vegas, Nevada, 5.75" h. $15-20.

Not to be outdone by private organizations and foreign powers, the U.S. State Department ordered Seneca crystal for thirty American embassies and consulates in 1944 and 1945. These embassies spanned the globe, taking Seneca glass to: Albania, Austria, the Belgian Congo, Belgium, Brazil, Bulgaria, Canada, Ceylon, Costa Rica, Czechoslovakia, Denmark, France, Gibraltar, Greece, Guatemala, Hungary, Iceland, India, Iraq, the Netherlands and the Netherlands West Indies, Nicaragua, Nigeria, Panama, the Philippines, Poland, Spain, the former USSR, and Yugoslavia. While searching for glassware for a special occasion in her favorite store, Eleanor Roosevelt chose stems in an obsolete Seneca pattern, being sold at the reduced price of twenty-five cents a piece. These she chose over patterns offered by the staff from famous firms, expensive glasswares priced in excess of fifty dollars a dozen. Mrs. Roosevelt used her bargain Seneca glassware at a State dinner held in honor of England's King George VI. (Fleming Associates 1986)

Nor would Mrs. Roosevelt be the last person associated with the White House to order Seneca glass. Peach champagne glasses in the Epicure pattern were purchased for Vice President Lyndon Johnson by his wife. Each glass was decorated with the vice president's initials, LBJ, and a Stetson hat. In fact, between the Seneca Glass Company and the Morgantown Glassware Guild, Morgantown (West Virginia) firms had the Kennedy administration's top executives covered. Glassware from the Guild was chosen by Jacqueline Kennedy for use in the White House. After filling that order, the Morgantown Glassware Guild promptly offered the Kennedy's choice in glassware to the public as the President's House line. (Six 1991, 77-78; Snyder 1998, 45-46)

Tag, no date.

Line 1962, cordial, "LBJ" (Lyndon B. Johnson) initials in a Stetson "Open Road" hat, Continental pattern, 3.75" h. $10-15.

For nearly a century, the Seneca Glass Company produced quality glassware for the rich and famous and for the average American citizen with above-average taste. Today, Seneca glassware is highly prized and actively sought by an ever-growing group of collectors with impeccable taste. What follows is a survey of the wide variety of enduring Seneca glasswares available to collectors today.

Stem 190, water goblets, cut 190-2, with cut feet, 8" h. $50-60.

Line 476, cut 654: hollow stem champagne, 6" h. $60-70; wine, 6" h. $25-35; sherry, 5" h. $25-35; cordial, 4.75" h. $25-35; cocktail, 5.25" h. $25-35; tumblers, 5.5" and 5.25" h. $15-20 ea.; Old Fashion, 3.25" h. $25-35; whiskey, 2.5" h. $25-35; finger bowl, 4.5" h. $25-35; tankard, 9" h. $60-70.

Line 190, cut 190-7: water goblet, 8" h. $25-35; iced tea, 6.75" h. $25-35; champagne, 6" h. $25-35; hollow stem honeycomb cut champagne, 5.25" h. $35-50; cocktail, 5.25" h. $25-35; juice/claret, 4.75" h. $25-35; and plate, 8.5" h. $10-15.

Bitter bottles, cut 76, 7" h. $65-75 ea.
Line 1202: compote, 6.75" h. $35-50; low wine, 3.25" h. $15-25; creamer, 4.5" h. $60-70; decanter, with cut stopper, 9.5" h. $60-70.

~Glassware Terminology~

Before plunging deep into the world of Seneca glass, it is useful to take a moment and define the terms that will be used throughout this text. **Glass** itself is well defined by Robert S. Weiner, in his dissertation *The Location and Distribution of the Glass Industry of Ohio, Pennsylvania, and West Virginia*: "an amorphous substance, usually transparent or translucent, consisting ordinarily of a mixture of silicates . . . Most glass is made by fusing together some form of silica, as sand, an alkali, as pot ash or soda, and some other base, as lime or lead oxide." (Weiner 1949, 2)

The glass produced at Seneca is **handmade, mold blown glass**, although the company seems to have been reluctant to mention the fact that molds were used to shape the glass. This glassware type was produced by first gathering a small, molten blob of glass on the end of a hollow pipe or rod. Blowing through the pipe and manipulating it in specific ways, a glass worker next preshapes the slowly cooling, glowing mass. The blower then inserts the preshaped "gather" into an iron mold—a mold that a skilled Seneca artisan had produced. Blowing into the pipe forces the hot glass to conform to the shape of the inside of the mold. Depending on the specific object being produced, several operations may follow. For example, on stemware, the molding of the stem and foot might be done with forms and paddles. Once an item is formed, it is *annealed* (reheated and allowed to cool gradually and uniformly to avoid shattering the glass) in an oven called a *lehr*. The cooled object is then sent on for finishing operations, including the removal of excess glass, grinding, and polishing.

Assorted finishing tools. *Courtesy of the Seneca Center and Riverfront Museums, Inc.*

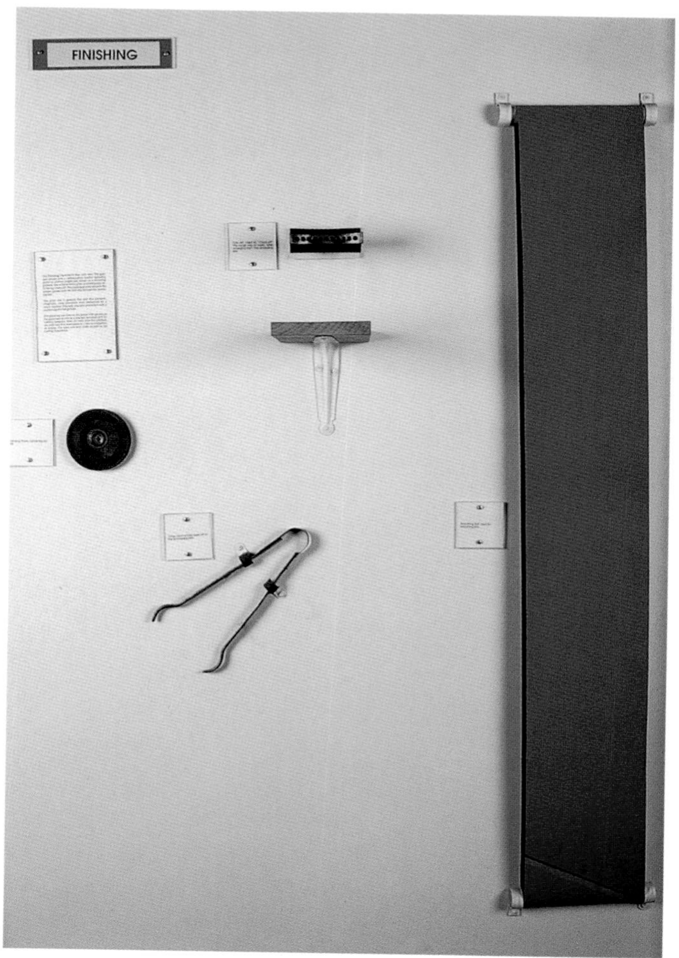

Gathering rods, used to gather molten glass for pressed ware. *Left:* white is unused, covered with fired clay ball. *Right:* red is used for ruby glass. *Courtesy of the Seneca Center and Riverfront Museums, Inc.*

Gathering rod *(left)*, used to gather amber glass; punty rod *(right)*, used to gather small amount of glass for a foot (base). *Courtesy of the Seneca Center and Riverfront Museums, Inc.*

Grinding wheels, used for cutting and smoothing crystal, made of sandstone and carborundum, ranging in size from 40 inches to 1 inch. *Courtesy of the Seneca Center and Riverfront Museums, Inc.*

Display of optic mold, used to make 20 optic pattern, hand cut from carbon rod. *Courtesy of the Seneca Center and Riverfront Museums, Inc.*

One glass "decorating" technique directly involving the shape of the interior of the mold itself is called the **optic**. The interior of the mold may be shaped in panels, pillars, spirals, swags, and/or other interesting shapes. These shapes become part of the shape of the body of the glass which is formed in an **optic mold**. The Seneca Glass Company used this technique to good effect, creating a variety of pleasing optics.

Stem 463, brandy snifter, palm optic, 22 oz., 5.75" h. $5-10.

The mold blown glass process used extensively by Seneca and others of the day differs from that of companies producing **machine made glass**. In 1972, the United States Tariff Commission, while studying claims from glass companies that foreign competitors were driving them from the marketplace, defined machine made glass as: "molten glass . . . fed in a continuous stream into a forming machine containing the molds; thus machine-made glassware is produced on a volume basis." (United States Tariff Commission 1972, A-1-2; Delores 1986).

Some of Seneca's specific glassware forms included goblets, sherbets, tall sherbets or champagnes, cocktails, oyster cocktails, sherries, wine glasses, clarets, and cordial glasses classified as "**stemware**;" ice teas, hi-balls, Old Fashioneds, juices, and water glasses grouped as "**tumblers**;" along with a variety of "**decorative glasswares**" or "**artwares**," including bowls, candleholders, and vases.

From *Catalog No. R83*, pg. 11.

From *Catalog No. R83*, pg. 6.

Assortment of line 180, cut 717: cordial, 4.5" h. $25-30; wine, 4.875" h. $25-30; champagne, 5.375" h. $25-30; Old Fashion, 3.5" h. $25-30; tumblers, footed, 5", 4.5", 4.875", 3.5" h. $20-25 ea.; tumblers, flared and straight, 5.5" h. $15-20.

Goblets were produced in three basic bowl shapes: the **bell**, **chalice**, and **tulip** shapes. In the bell shape, the rim of the bowl flares outward. The chalice bowl rim is straight. The rim of the tulip shape bowl turns inward. Stems on these goblets could have either been drawn from part of the goblet body, or molded and added to the bowl. Sometimes these stems featured creative and decorative twists or bubbles. (Manning 1984, 42)

Grouping of stemware showing the variety of cut stems and bowls.

Water goblet, cut 1401, with a cut stem, 8.25" h. $25-30.

Water goblet, cut 1401, with a straight stem, 7.5" h. $15-20.

Wine, cut 1454 Grande Baroque pattern, 5.125" h. NP.

Assorted cordials, 4.5" to 4.75" h., showing various cut and stems: cut 1446 Wicker pattern; stem 476, cut 476-2; cut 43, stem 982 (frosted); cut 1073 Moderne pattern, stem 476; cut 476-2, stem 476. *Left to right:* $20-25, $25-30, $15-20, $25-30, $25-30.

Stem 77 (twisted): wine, 5.75" h.; wine, 6.125" h.; cocktail, 4" h.; brandy, 4.75" h. $10-15 ea.

~Manufacturing Techniques~

Working in cooperation with the Seneca Glass Company, the Morgantown Glassware Guild (originally the Morgantown Glass Works), Davis-Lynch Glass Company, and the Beaumont Company, William J. Aull, Jr. provides a detailed account of how handmade, mold blown glassware was produced in his work *Sand, fire n' things*. Knowing exactly how glassware was produced will not only help you to better appreciate the ware, it also will provide you with insights helpful in identifying Seneca glasswares, and differentiating their mold blown products from those produced using other techniques, or by other firms.

To successfully produce quality glassware, clean silica-sand, extracted from rock and iron free, was required. Most of Seneca's sand was mined from West Virginia's Eastern Panhandle region. This silica-sand was shipped dry in closed railroad box cars to the plant, where it was stored carefully to avoid contamination. Soda-ash was added to the sand to encourage it to fuse more readily into glass. Various chemicals, including potash and nitrate of soda, were added to the mix to improve the working qualities of the glass. Additional ingredients were also added to set the coloration, clarity, and strength of the glass. Once mixed, this combination of sand and chemicals was referred to as a "batch."

A wide variety of materials could be used to change the color of the glass. Copper was used to produce a red. A deep ruby-red was produced by adding a selenium-cadmium mixture to the batch. This mix would initially create a yellow colored glass; however, when reheated it would "flash" into the ruby-red color. Mr. Aull also mentions some very unusual materials once used to color glass. For example, buffalo bones are no longer used because, they, "...as we all know, are not easily obtained in quantity. Another color required a twenty-dollar gold piece to be dissolved in acid and poured over the batch. This produced a beautiful purple-ruby color of glass. The Government now frowns on this use of their money, so gold chloride is substituted." (Aull 1965, 3)

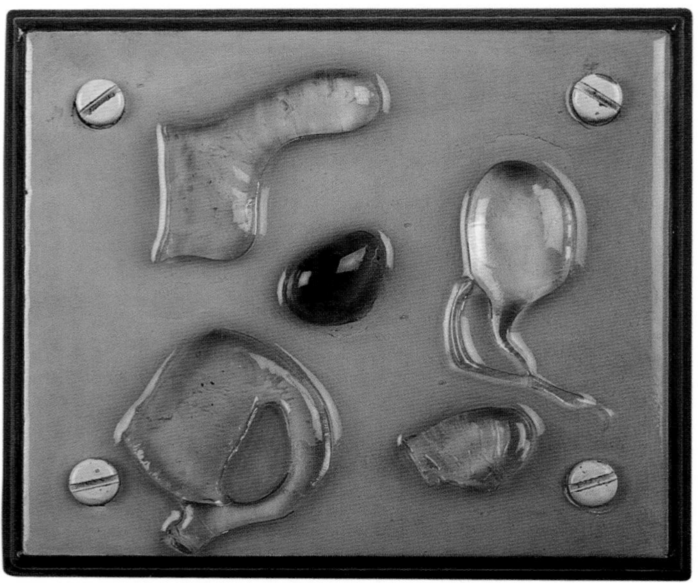

Glass samples taken from the pot to determine quality, color, and clarity. *Courtesy of the Seneca Center and Riverfront Museums, Inc.*

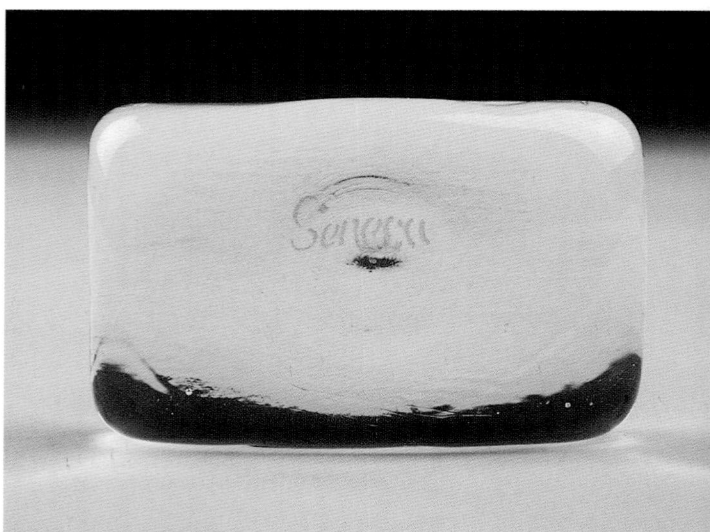

Above and left: A wide variety of materials were used to change the color of the glass. Seneca color block examples.

Snap-up tool, used to grab or hold the piece of glass after it had been blown or formed into a shape; at Seneca, the tool was primarily used over the "glory hole," which was a separate small furnace used to make flashed ruby glass. *Courtesy of the Seneca Center and Riverfront Museums, Inc.*

After the color of the glass was determined and the coloration process completed, broken glass referred to as "cullet" was added to the batch. Introducing cullet into the mix, melted the batch into glass more quickly. To melt the now thoroughly mixed and complete batch into glass, the prepared batch was shoveled into refractory pots made of clay. These pots were heated in the factory's closed, natural gas burning furnace for twenty-five to thirty-eight hours. Temperatures within the furnace were around 2500 degrees Fahrenheit. Over time, the batch melted into a glowing hot liquid glass ready to be worked by Seneca's craftsmen and women.

Cullet, excess glass that was taken from the pot when cleaned. Some cullet was reused and some was sold to marble factories and other glass factories. *Courtesy of the Seneca Center and Riverfront Museums, Inc.*

It took a team ranging in size from three to fifteen people to successfully complete a single piece of Seneca glassware. These teams were referred to as shops, and each shop member had a specialty. To begin the process of transforming molten glass into a useful vessel, the "gathering boy" (an adult whose title was created during the era when young boys began their apprenticeships in glassmaking as gatherers) took the "blow pipe"—a five foot long, hollow steel rod that tapered at one end into a conical head and had a rubber handle on the other—inserted it into the furnace, and touched the tapered end to the liquid glass. Rotating the pipe against the surface of the glass, he gathered glass on the end of the pipe. The amount of glass gathered depended upon the size of the vessel being produced. It took sound judgment and years of practice to accurately determine when enough glass was gathered.

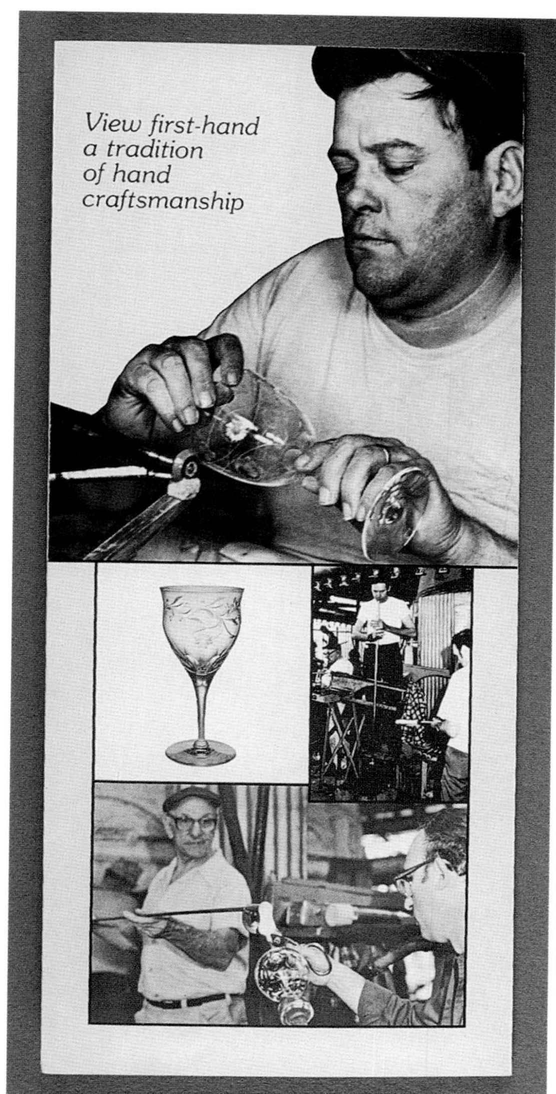

The various steps in the glassmaking process. From Seneca™ Crystal Inc. Factory, Outlet, & Tours brochure, no date.

Blow pipe, used to blow air into a molten glob of glass. *Courtesy of the Seneca Center and Riverfront Museums, Inc.*

Once the molten glass was gathered on the end of the blow pipe, the gathering boy laid the hot ball of glass onto a slab of polished steel called a "marver." There he turned the blow pipe, packing and shaping the glass quickly. Once satisfied, he blew into the pipe and handed the prepared blow pipe over to the blower who would see to the molding of the glass.

If the item to be produced was larger and required additional glass than was currently on the pipe, the pipe was given to the "ball boy" (a man or a woman) who first blew into the pipe. This created a bubble in the ball of heated glass. Once formed, the glass was handed to the "blocker," whose job it was to see that the glass was in an appropriate final form for the object to be blown. The blocker reinserted the glass into the furnace and more glass was gathered on top of the preexisting ball. Once the blocker had a ball of glass on the end of the pipe in a size and shape he deemed acceptable, he handed off the pipe and glass to the blower.

Glass blowers were large men who stood on raised platforms when transforming hot glass blobs into recognizable objects. Oscar DuBois, a glass cutter who worked for several Morgantown area glass firms for many years, described the blowers as "big guys 175 to 180 [lbs.], or sometimes six-footers who weighed 200 pounds." Mr. DuBois further related that blowing was a taxing job: "Most blowers quit by the time they were 55. They just ran out of wind. Some maybe stretched it out to 60." (Aull 1965, 2-6; Julian 1980, 44)

When a blower felt the hot glass was properly prepared, he lowered it into an open iron mold. Once the glass was secured into place by the mold boy, the blower would begin to blow into the far end of the pipe, expanding the hot glass to fill the mold and conform to the mold's shape.

Two types of molds were generally used, depending on the shape of the vessel being blown. Objects with irregular shapes were blown into polished cast iron molds. The hot glass came into direct contact with the interior surfaces of the mold and mold seams were left behind on the glass. However, if an object was to be round, a "paste" mold was used. A paste mold, while still made of cast iron, had a cork dust paste coating on the interior surfaces of the mold. This paste acted as an interior lining. The blower would rotate the expanding glass sphere within the circular paste mold. As the rotating hot glass came in contact with the lining, the revolving action wiped away any imperfections in the hot glass.

Cordial mold, cast iron, used to make 3005 line of crystal stemware. *Courtesy of the Seneca Center and Riverfront Museums, Inc.*

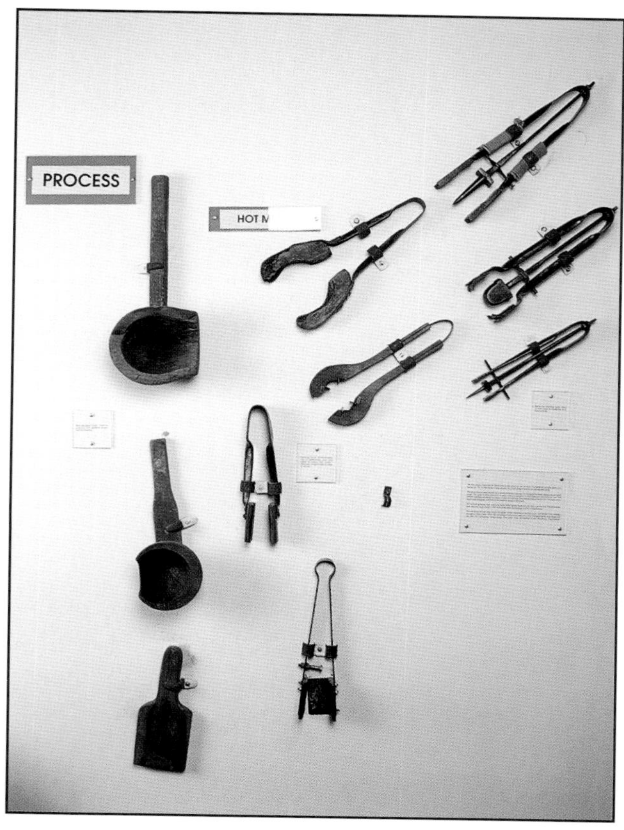

Display of wet wooden forms, used to produce the general shape before blowing; forming tongs, used in general forming of glassware and used to carry hot ware; bottle-top forming tools, used to form tops of medicine and liquor bottles. *Courtesy of the Seneca Center and Riverfront Museums, Inc.*

Once an item had its shape and was removed from the mold, the excess glass connecting the object to the blow pipe was either cut away with hand shears while the glass was still warm and malleable, or cracked off with a tool resembling a chisel once the object had cooled and hardened. It all depended upon the object being produced.

From Seneca™ Crystal Inc. Factory, Outlet, & Tours brochure, no date.

Tin mold, used to make impression of large bowls. *Courtesy of the Seneca Center and Riverfront Museums, Inc.*

Crack-off tools, used to crack off pieces of ware from the blow pipe. *Courtesy of the Seneca Center and Riverfront Museums, Inc.*

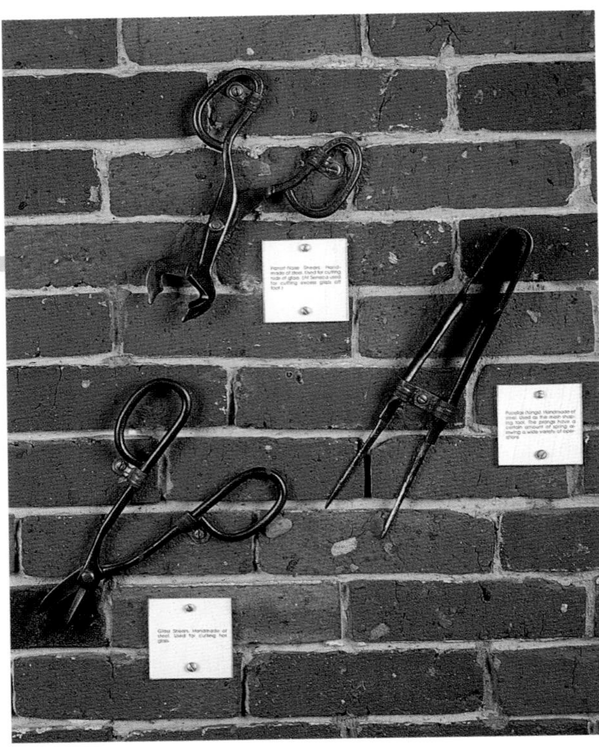

Display of parrot-nose shears *(upper left)*, steel, used for cutting rods of glass, at Seneca used for cutting excess glass off foot; glass shears *(lower left)*, steel, used for cutting hot glass; pucellas, or tongs *(right)*, steel, used as the main shaping tools. *Courtesy of the Seneca Center and Riverfront Museums, Inc.*

Cooling the glass was the next step in the process. However, the glass could not be allowed to cool at its own rate or it would shatter under the stress. Instead, the now cooling glass was sent on a trip through a tunnel-shaped kiln referred to as a lehr. Within the lehr, temperatures were reduced gradually at a controlled pace from one end of the lehr to the other, preventing disaster. This gradual cooling process, known as annealing, strengthened the glass. (Aull 1965, 2-6)

Display of foot gauge *(upper left)*, used to check the diameter and general shape of the foot; and two carrying tools *(below)*, used to carry crystal to the annealing lehr: single pong *(on top)* used for stemware, and triple prong *(on bottom)* used for punchware (i.e., Driftwood Casual series). *Courtesy of the Seneca Center and Riverfront Museums, Inc.*

Detail showing carrying tools: single and triple prong. *Courtesy of the Seneca Center and Riverfront Museums, Inc.*

Now the undecorated glass objects referred to as "blanks" could be decorated in any number of ways, depending on the type of object and its intended market. The Seneca Glass Company specialized in transforming crystal blanks into fine cut glass.

Cut 777, brandy, 5.125" h. $50-65; wine, 6.425" h. $50-65; low cocktail, 3.5" h. $50-65; water goblet, 7" h. $70-80.

One last observation from Mr. DuBois before moving onto the discussion of glass decorations employed by Seneca. Mr. DuBois's comparison of the blowers and the cutters provides some insight into the internal politics of a glass factory. Of the blower, Mr. DuBois stated, "the blower was the best job in the industry requiring big men with an artist's touch." Of the cutters, a job Oscar DuBois performed himself for many years, he observed: "The cutters sort of dressed up a little better. They worked days . . . They were sort of what you might call the white collar group . . . The cutting was very difficult. It was kept in families." (Julian 1980, 44-45)

~Decorating Techniques~ Surface Decorating Techniques

Almost every glass decorating technique available to twentieth-century glass manufacturers was employed by Seneca. However, explored here are those most frequently used by Seneca. Coloring glass has already been touched upon in the Manufacturing section and will not be repeated here. One should note, however, that while Seneca offered colored glassware by the 1920s, their most notable colored glassware lines were produced from the 1950s onward. During the 1970s, the firm produced some truly unusual colored glasswares such as the Artichoke line. The company would also produce a line of collector's bells during this period, bells produced in lead crystal featuring cut decorations.

ARTICHOKE
by SENECA

ARTICHOKE
1985 Goblet
Delphine Blue
6⅜" hi.

ARTICHOKE
1985 Goblet
Crystal
6⅜" hi.

ARTICHOKE
1985 Goblet
Crystal/Black Foot
6⅜" hi.

ARTICHOKE
1985 Goblet
Moss Green
6⅜" hi.

Seneca's new ARTICHOKE Pattern is mouth blown, hand made and hand finished, and available in the following colors: Brown, Crystal, Crystal with Black Foot, Delphine Blue, Moss Green and Yellow.

The ARTICHOKE Pattern #1985 available in the following items:

Goblet
Juice/Wine
Beverage
Hi Ball
On The Rocks
Plate

3

From *Supplement Catalogue No. 78*, pg. 3.

Revolving brass pedestal, used to mark the design lines with red-lead paint. *Courtesy of the Seneca Center and Riverfront Museums, Inc.*

Cutting

Seneca produced fine cut glass in abundance. As time passed, more space on the glass was left open and uncut as compared with their earlier wares. Also, over time the cuts began to appear softer and more unpolished. (Six 1991, 74, 78)

Prior to glass cutting, selectors inspected finished blown wares. Once defective items were removed, the remaining wares were sent on to the markers. Markers used either red lead and oil of turpentine or stencil ink to mark the general outlines of the pattern on the glass for the cutters. Lines and dots were used to indicate exactly where the cutters were to place the designs.

Marked wares were sent on to flute cutters, miter cutters, or stopperers. The **flute cutters** cut flutes into the bases of glasses by holding a glass against a horizontal wheel made of either sandstone or aloxite. Aloxite was a crystalline alumina abrasive containing small impurities.

Miter cutters produced a variety of designs using high speed aloxite wheels with edges "dressed" (that is wheels with edges angled in specific shapes) to create desired types of cuts. Between 100 and 150 different wheels were available to Seneca cutters. Water was continuously dripping on the wheel during the cutting operation to increase the speed of the cutting. (Bureau of Industrial Hygiene 1937-38, 37-38)

Cutters were paid by the piece, so it behooved them to work rapidly. To that end, an experienced cutter would work on a box containing 35 pieces as one time. The cutter would select a wheel required for a particular portion of the decoration and then would use it on all 35 pieces at the same time. With every change of the wheel, a new part of the pattern was applied to all 35 items at once, moving the process forward at a rapid pace. Pattern elements that worked well in cut glass included hatching (vertical, diamond or pineapple), starbursts, flowers, branches, butterflies, and birds. (Manning 1984, 41-42)

Stopperers, or **stopper grinders**, placed a stopper in a lathe (a device designed to hold and rotate the stopper). While holding the bottle, the stopperer would grind the stopper into the bottle with the help of emery dust. At times the stopper and bottle neck were left rough, or "frosted," following the emery grinding. Otherwise, they were polished with fine sand, producing a clear and transparent neck and stopper.

After the cutting was complete, the glass was either polished by a hand polisher or it was given an acid polish. To acid polish a piece, it was dipped into a hydrofluoric and sulfuric acid solution, until the rough cuts were polished. Pure hydrofluoric acid was not used, as it would not produce a satisfactory final polish. The acid polisher wore rubber gloves, an apron, and boots, and handled racks of glassware, being careful never to allow his hands to come in contact with the acid solution. The acid vats were hooded and exhaust fans removed the fumes. Following the acid bath polishing, the glassware was carefully washed and polished with a cloth.

Hand polishing was accomplished with a cork wheel coated with pumice paste. The polisher used this wheel to polish each cut on every item. This was a labor-intensive job requiring more time than the actual cutting had originally taken. If the glass was pressed against the wheel too hard and became heated, smears or dark spots could be created around the cuts. These imperfections would require subsequent removal by a buffer using a hard pressed felt wheel and putty. The putty was made from a special mixture of lead and very fine pumice.

On hollow wares, a rough spot was left on the base of the glass where the ware had been stuck to the hollow blow pipe, or "punty." This spot was ground off by a punty grinder or punty bottom boy using a steel wheel and powdered emery. The emery was kept wet during the punty grinding.

Once the hand polished ware was finished, it was washed in soap suds and polished with a cloth. (Bureau of Industrial Hygiene 1937-38, 37-38)

Creating a Cut Glass Pattern

Much careful consideration went into the development of each and every Seneca cut glass pattern. A cut glass pattern was usually developed in the following manner. Initially, a member of the sales team would suggest a pattern design needed in the market place. The manager and several cutters would get together and discuss the possibilities for the design. Once the ideas were gathered, one cutter would cut a glass to match the design. The glass cut would be the largest form in the line, such as a water goblet. The group would meet again and the pattern would be refined and cut again. Once the finial form for the pattern was agreed upon, a cutter would take the final model and cut about a dozen more just like it. At this point, careful notes were taken concerning how long it took to finish the pattern. These notes would be used to help set the selling price for wares decorated in this new pattern.

Once completed, the models were passed out among the other cutters, who practiced creating the new patterns on glass seconds. Seconds were items flawed in some way, making them good candidates as practice pieces. Once the pattern was successfully produced, it was adapted to smaller sized glasswares. Only when the cutting staff was comfortable with the new pattern and their execution of it was it ready to be offered to the public.

Samples were handed over to sales. If the pattern was then well received, it was assigned a number used to identify it in the plant and became part of the Seneca Glass Company's open stock, available to the public for sale. (Manning 1984, 45)

Etching

Both needle and plate etching were acid etching techniques. As with the cut glass, glass companies assigned specific numbers to each of their etchings for identification. Glassware companies also frequently contracted out to other firms to provide etched decorations for the company's glass blanks. (Wiley 1996, 3)

Assortment of stemware with deep etch 608: stem 81, wine, 5" h. $15-20; stem 31, grapefruit bowl, 5.5" h. $15-20; stem 300, hollow stem champagne, cut 43, 5.25" h. $25-30.

Detail of deep etch 608.

Needle Etching

This process requires both a complex and intricate machine and a skilled setter capable of properly adjusting the machinery to produce the desired pattern. The first step in the needle etching process was to dip the ware to be etched in wax. The "dipper" performs this necessary first step. The wax coated glass was then taken to the needle machine. The operator carefully placed the ware upside down on a rubber cushioned plate where it was held fast by suction. The operator lowered the machine's arms, each with needles fastened to one end, against the glass and turned on the machine. The glass slowly rotated while the needles traced the pattern into the wax.

Once the pattern was inscribed into the wax, the glass was removed from the machine and a touch-up girl repaired any spots where the wax coating had been damaged by handling. After the wax coating was repaired, the glass was taken to the dipping room, where an acid etcher immersed the ware in a hydrofluoric acid bath. The exposed glass was eaten away by the acid, transferring the design etched in the wax to the glass. The length of time the glass was to remain in the bath was determined by the depth of the etching required.

Once removed from the bath, the glass was taken to a steamer. The wax was steamed off. Finally a polish girl polished the needle etch decorated glass with sawdust and then with a cloth (Bureau of Industrial Hygiene 1937-38, 38-39).

Plate Etching

Before it ever appeared on a piece of glass, a plate etch design was first etched onto a steel plate. While a few glass plants etched their own plates, this job was generally handled by an outside firm.

The transfer man, or printer, transferred the pattern from the steel plate to paper. To accomplish this transfer, the transfer man first warmed the steel plate and placed it, design side up, on a solid table. A mixture of lamp black and melted wax was poured over the plate. Excess wax was removed with a "printer's plate," a scraper with a broad, thin, flexible steel blade. The transfer man then placed a very thin transfer paper over the plate and pressed it onto the plate with a steel roller. Before the paper was used, the side to be printed was coated with a soft soap solution so the wax would not come in direct contact with the paper. This ensured that the paper could be easily removed once the design had been transferred to the glass.

When the transfer paper was removed from the steel plate, the wax adhered to it, leaving the design outline in the wax. The portion of the design to be etched remained wax free.

The printed paper was taken to the print cutter, who cut away the extra paper and gave the design to the "putting-on girl." The putting-on girl placed the printed side of the paper against the glassware and pressed it down smoothly by hand. The piece was then sent on to the "rubbing-down girl" who rubbed the paper with a stiff brush to ensure that every part of the design was in close contact with the glass. At that point, the "taking-off girl" removed the paper from the glass with lukewarm water, leaving the wax behind on the glass. The taking-off girl had to be careful that the water was not too hot or the wax design would melt away in the bath.

From the taking-off girl, the glass went to the "touching-up girl." This individual covered the rest of the glass with wax, leaving only the design wax free. The well-waxed glass was then sent on to the acid dipping room where it was dipped in a hydrofluoric acid bath. After the bath, the wax was removed by steaming, and the now etched glass was polished, first with sawdust and then with a cloth. (Bureau of Industrial Hygiene 1937-38, 39-40)

Sandblasting

As with the etching techniques, glasswares to be decorated using the sandblasting method were first thoroughly dipped in wax. Once the wax had hardened, a pattern was cut into the wax, laying bare the glass directly beneath the pattern. Once the pattern was complete and any damage to the surround wax had been repaired, the wax coated object was placed in a sandblasting machine. A concentrated sand stream cut the design into the portions of the glass revealed when the pattern was cut into the wax coating. The longer the glassware was exposed to the flying sand, the deeper the pattern would be cut into the glass. Once the pattern was cut, an acid bath smoothed the cuts. Then the wax was removed and the decorated glass received a final hand polishing. (Six 1991, 73, 76-77)

Metallic Decorations

Gold, silver, and platinum were all applied to glassware in addition to vitrified colors and lusters. There were two types of metallic decoration, bright and burnished. Burnished metals were generally supplied by manufacturers in a paste form and applied with a brush. After firing, the metal was burnished using burnishing sand, a fine, round grained sand that would not scratch the metal.

The bright metal was a resinate dissolved in turpentine and lavender oil, containing a small amount of rhodium that caused the metal to turn bright when fired. This eliminated the need for burnishing. As with the burnished metal, this resinate mix was applied with a brush.

Sandblasting templates, used for etching patterns on glass, handmade of tin prior to 1920. *Courtesy of the Seneca Center and Riverfront Museums, Inc.*

Electroplating was also used to produce fine decorative effects. Electroplated designs were first printed and fired onto the glass with a paste mixture containing precipitating silver flux and oil. All of the disparate parts of the decoration were connected with an electric current source. The ware was immersed in an electroplating bath, and a deposit of pure silver was plated over the fired design. This plating was polished and frequently given a coating of rhodium to prevent tarnishing (Bureau of Industrial Hygiene 1937-38, 44).

Cordials with gold-band rims, 3.75" and 4" h. *Left to right:* $20-25, $15-20, $15-20.

Color Banding, Lining, and Painting

Despite that similarities between these three processes, they should not be confused with metallic band decorations applied with an electroplating process.

Color banding materials were very finely ground and thoroughly dry. They were usually mixed, a small amount at a time, with fat oil of turpentine or oil of copaiba. Decorators then applied the color to glassware with a fine brush. The use of a decorating wheel allowed horizontal lines to be applied with greater speed.

Machines were developed to apply simpler types of **linings** (bandings applied mechanically by rotating wheels or discs.) For machine use, the color was mixed with water and alcohol, or water and glycerine. It was then applied to rotating glassware with tracking wheels or discs.

Painted designs were often produced by first printing the outline of the design onto the glass with a steel plate transfer process and then filling in the open spaces of the design by hand, using a variety of colors. (Bureau of Industrial Hygiene 1937-38, 41-42)

~Decorations Within the Glass~

Moving inward, here are decorations that were molded into the body of the glass.

Optics, Decorations From the Mold

As previously discussed, an optic is a decoration molded into the body of the glassware. The decoration is transferred from the interior of the two-piece iron mold, where it was originally created, to the body of the ware as the hot blown glass expanded to fill the interior of the mold.

Line 9491, iced tea, palm optic, 7" h. $8-10.

~About the Values~

The values found in the captions are in United States dollars. Prices vary immensely based on the location of the market and the enthusiasms of the collecting community. Prices in the Midwest differ from those on either coast, and those at specialty shows or auctions will differ from values in dealers' shops.

All of these factors make it impossible to create absolutely accurate value listings, but a guide to realistic pricing may be offered. These values are *not* provided to set prices in the collectibles marketplace, but rather to give the reader a realistic idea of what one might expect to pay for Seneca glass in mint condition.

History

~Glass History~

Being aware of the company history and the changes in glass design over the decades will help collectors to identify and date Seneca glassware more accurately and confidently.

During the nineteenth century, improvements in transportation via canals, railroads, and steamboats opened new glass markets for the glass industry in the United States, particularly in the South and Midwest. Glass manufacturers drifted westward, removing themselves from the Eastern Seaboard and establishing factories west of the Allegheny Mountains. The first flint glass (lead glass) works were established in Pittsburgh between 1808 and 1814. The Zanesville Glass Manufacturing Company of Zanesville, Ohio, followed in 1815. Entering the industry a little later, a flint and cut glass plant was established in Wheeling, West Virginia, in 1831.

With this westward movement came new and more efficient fuels to fire the glass furnaces and increase production. By 1830, coal had almost completely replaced wood. Natural gas was first discovered in Pennsylvania, in 1859, and soon replaced coal as the fuel of choice to fire furnaces. As the years rolled by, additional natural gas wells sprung up in western Pennsylvania, West Virginia, Ohio, and Indiana. As the gas wells of western Pennsylvania were depleted, glass plants moved into West Virginia, Ohio, and Indiana to take advantage of fresh gas deposits there. In fact, during this period, the developing glass industry followed the newly discovered gas wells like birds following a trail of bread crumbs.

A large concentration of glass factories developed in West Virginia, Pennsylvania, and Ohio, located roughly between Charleston, Toledo, and Port Allegheny. Within this "glass triangle," the heaviest concentration of factories was located in the northern and western counties of West Virginia and the western counties of Pennsylvania. Out of the factories in this tri-state region sprung all types of glass, from handmade, mold blown tablewares, to mass-produced bottles and free blown art glass. (Weiner 1949, 8, 20-21; Piña 1995, 6)

Rear view of Seneca Glass factory complex, c. 1902. Note B & O train cars in the foreground. Photographer Wm. Earl Rumsey. *Courtesy of the Seneca Center and Riverfront Museums, Inc.*

The factors determining the location of these glass factories included proximity to raw materials, fuel, and abundant labor, along with access to large markets through reliable transportation systems. Of all these factors, close proximity to a large deposit of high quality glass sand was paramount. Within the "glass triangle," there were several major high grade glass sand deposits. One was located in Berkley Springs, West Virginia, and another was found in Mapleton, Pennsylvania. These sand deposits are identified as Oriskany Quartzite. They were deposited in this region some 350 million years ago during the Devonian period as a blanket of white marine sandstone seventy-five to one hundred feet thick. The Oriskany deposits provide not only high quality glass sand, but natural gas as well, meeting two of the criteria necessary to establish a successful glass factory.

The Seneca Glass Company also received quality glass sand from both Hancock, Maryland, and a nearby outcropping in Deckers Creek Valley, West Virginia. The close proximity of the Deckers Creek Valley deposit was significant. There Seneca could obtain the necessary sands for less than a third of the price they were required to pay for shipments from the previous Seneca County, Ohio, location. (Weiner 1949, 25-26; Core 1982, 31, 202)

Glass factories also needed to be located near their consumer markets. Glass containers and inexpensive pressed or blown glasswares are bulky objects prone to breakage. None of the early twentieth century glass factory in America could afford to support the high distribution costs incurred by long distance shipping. The factories of the glass triangle were located in the middle of America's former manufacturing belt (today's "rust" belt), where in 1940 roughly 46 percent of the American population lived and worked.

Finally, successful glass factories were located near reliable transportation resources. For the Seneca Glass Company and other factories of the glass triangle, this transportation source was the railroad. The northeastern quadrant of the United States had the heaviest concentration of railroad networks anywhere within the forty-eight contiguous states. These rail lines provided the glass factories with ready access to their raw materials, to other industrial regions, and to the large urban consumer markets.

Nineteenth-century technological innovations also accelerated production in the glass plants. By 1850, iron molds were improving glass production, ensuring a greater uniformity among glasswares while reducing the time necessary to create a finished product. Designs carved or cast into the insides of the molds could even imitate the look of expensive hand-cut glass. Glass furnaces were also increasing in size and quality, allowing for higher glass output, a faster working pace, and more routine tasks for workers to perform. As iron molds and improved furnaces became commonplace, glass blowers were no longer required to blow and shape each piece by hand. A number of additional workers now handled the glass both before and after blowing. Among them were gatherers, cracking-off boys, warming-in boys, carrying-in boys, and mold-boys.

As the nineteenth century drew to a close (and the Seneca Glass Company moved to Morgantown), the glass industry was rapidly expanding. Consumer demand was on the rise as well. Machinery in the factories was increasing the rate of production and lessening the effects of labor scarcities in some regions. The glass factories themselves were expanding in size and were employing larger numbers of workers than ever before. The glasswares produced by these expanding firms were changing as well, exhibiting new ranges of imaginative shapes, colors, and functions at the dawn of the twentieth century. (Weiner 1949, 21-22, 36, 42; Zembala 1984, 367)

~Late Nineteenth & Twentieth Century Glassware Design~

In the early decades of the twentieth century, the Seneca Glass Company emphasized their production of elaborate, expensive, crystal clear glass patterns. However, many glass companies were following trends toward simplified and more colorful glass forms. Bearing this in mind, Seneca would follow suit and produce some of the simpler and more colorful wares as well. An article from 1934 stated: "Most factories had kept in mind the great popularity of the buffet supper and created many varieties of articles for the convenience—and pride—of the hostess at such a party." (*China, Glass and Lamps* 1934, 11-16)

Blown and pressed art glass would retain its popularity until around the beginning of the first world war. Brilliant and deeply cut glass, popular near the end of the nineteenth century, was continued in the early twentieth century; however, by the 1920s, this very expensive glassware would fade from the scene as economic depression loomed. Cut glass would not return to heightened popularity until the 1940s.

Handmade, mold blown glass and machine made glasswares were in direct competition for the consumer's dollars. By the 1930s, roughly half of all the glass produced in the United States would be entirely machine made.

Machine made "Depression glass" (produced from the 1920s onward to the beginning of World War II) glittered on the shelves of the "five and dime" stores around the country, providing consumers for the first time with useful, inexpensive, complete dinner services and matching serving pieces. Some of the patterns produced were similar in design to the more expensive patterns glass factories were also producing for their wealthier customers. (Phillips 1981, 206-208; Weatherman 1974, 8)

To survive in the competitive marketplace, glass factories had to appeal to a wide range of tastes. Colored glass drew attention in the 1920s and was much in demand in the 1930s. By 1935, roughly half the glass being produced sported colors. Colored glass during the Depression years was generally bright and cheerful. Art Deco colors and shapes were added to glassware lines in the 1930s as well.

The 1930s brought about another change that directly affected the glassware industry, the repeal of Prohibition (the 18th Amendment to the Constitution had been ratified January 16, 1919 and went into effect the following year). Edmondson Warrin expounded upon what the end of Prohibition would mean for the glassware industry in his article entitled "And Now—A Toast!"

He stated,

> With the repeal of the 18th amendment expected in a few weeks, we will come into a period of more dignified drinking. We will watch the bubbles rise in a beautiful champagne glass of fine crystal. Creators of fine things in glass will win a nation back to appreciate the bouquet, color and taste of fine wines.
>
> For this enjoyment we will need finer and more complete sets of glassware, correct glasses for sherry, champagne, Burgundy, white and red wines, Rhine wine and cordials. A woman's set of glassware will mean something to cherish and to show. The hostess in this new era will be deeply interested in what the merchant has to offer for her consideration. (Warrin 1933, 13 & 38)

From company brochure, no date.

The glasswares Mr. Warrin mentioned were strengths of the Seneca Glass Company, which no doubt took quick advantage of Prohibition's repeal.

Barware and kitchenware were important production items for factories in the 1930s and 1940s, as they could be produced in large quantities at low production costs. Refrigerator storage dishes and oven-proof glass cookware were introduced for the modern kitchen. At times, serving dishes and punch bowls were sold together with metal holders.

After World War II, during the 1940s, cut crystal stemware would return as a popular form, especially as gifts for the bride—a situation that worked well for Seneca Glass. During the 1940s and 1950s, one of the major trends developed by American glass designers involved the creation of free blown abstract forms similar to those of European glassmakers. Color, form, and texture all played significant parts in post-war era designs. Later examples of Seneca glasswares reflect this trend. Leslie Piña states: "The hills of West Virginia in the 1950s and 1960s were to American modern glass design what Murano or Orrefors were to European design" (Piña 1995, 6). Many innovative designs were produced in West Virginia during this time.

~The History of the Seneca Glass Company~

In 1896, five years into Seneca's establishment in the Fostoria Glass Company's factory building, the Seneca Glass Company was enticed away from Seneca County, Ohio, to Morgantown, West Virginia. Morgantown was an impressive city in the late nineteenth century and had plenty to offer the fledgling glass company. The city was home to over eighteen thousand individuals. Steam powered locomotives and packet boats delivered people and products regularly to and from this busy town nestled along the banks of the Monongahela River. A combination of natural gas and electricity lit the avenues from downtown to the periphery so well that the local paper proclaimed the city to be the best lit in the state. Local supplies of natural gas were available to power diverse and growing industries. And Morgantown's civic leaders were determined to make Morgantown an industrial powerhouse in the region.

To convince Seneca's management to move, a Morgantown investment firm offered the glass company a subsidy and free land upon which to build their plant. The property was located along the Monongahela River, providing all the water necessary to run a glass plant, along with direct access to steamboat lines. Additionally, rail transportation to Pittsburgh had just opened in 1894, and the railroad lines ran directly through the proposed factory site. Further sweetening the deal, the Baltimore and Ohio Railroad agreed to transfer all of Seneca's movable equipment from the Ohio factory to the new Morgantown location for free. (Robinson 1955, 95; Six 1991, 71)

Seneca Glass Company's management accepted the offer on June 18, 1896, agreeing to have the Morgantown Building and Investment Company construct the factory and a 14 pot glass furnace, a $20,000 project. The contractors agreed to have the facility ready for production in Morgantown on January 1, 1897. The *New Dominion* newspaper (so named to allow West Virginians to poke fun at Virginia, known as the "Old Dominion," from which West Virginia seceded during the American Civil War) described how Morgantown's officials benefited from Seneca as follows:

> By the present contract 250 people are employed. This business will necessitate them as soon as arrangements can be made to enlarge their factory to 28 shops, when their pay roll will show up in the neighborhood of 500 employees.

The Seneca Glass Company, located at Beechurst Avenue and 7th Street, was a success. The company's initial production was also described in the *New Dominion* in 1897:

> The output with the present working force in tumblers alone is 3,000 dozen per day. If the natural gas was to go off for one short hour while the glass was being tempered the firm would sustain a loss of $2000 . . . their specialties are water pitchers, water bottles, finger bowls, goblets, punch tumblers, sherbet glasses and all kinds of diminutive glasses for cordials. (Core 1982, 220)

Among Seneca's early wares were also bar bottles, covered candy jars, cream and sugar sets, nappies, plates, trays, and vases. A significant portion of the company's early production was dedicated to the manufacture of thin, etched tumblers used both in bars and as advertisements for a wide variety of organizations and products. (Page et al. 1995, viii)

Catalogue #2 showcases the early offerings of the Seneca Glass Company.

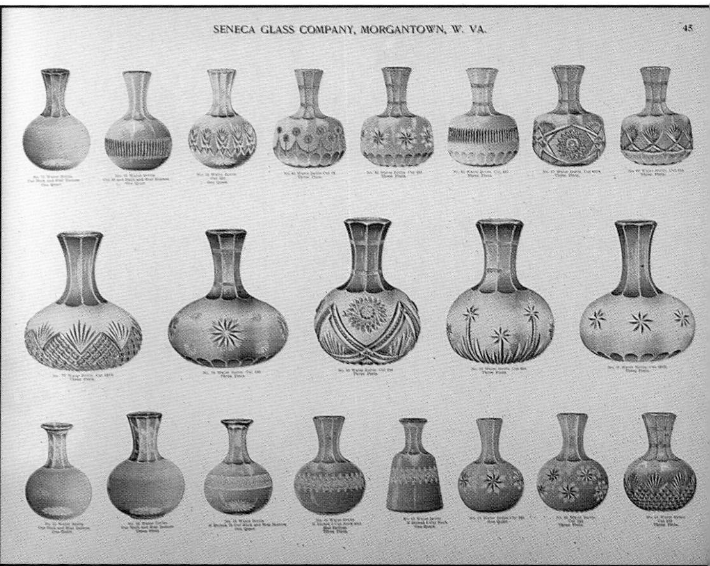

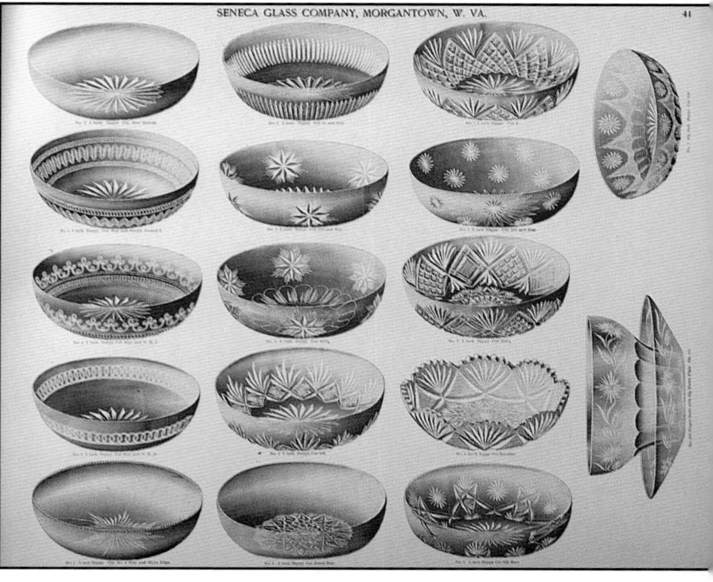

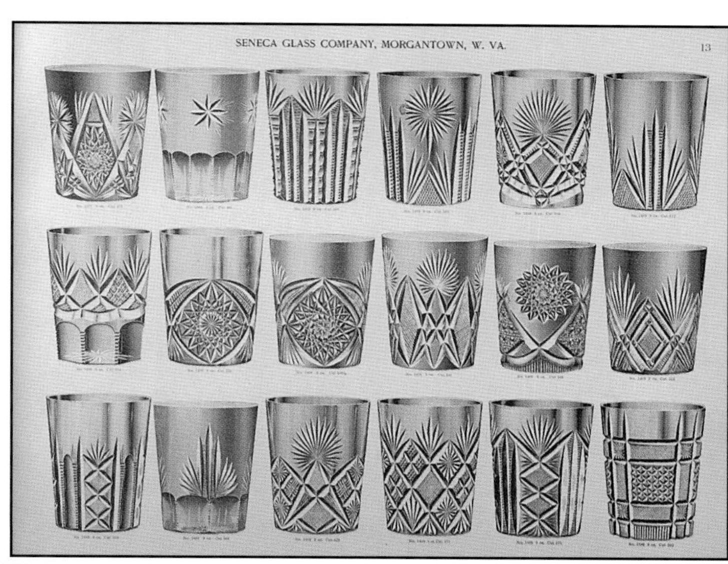

Advertising print blocks used during the 1890s and 1900s. *Courtesy of the Seneca Center and Riverfront Museums, Inc.*

With the initial success of the Seneca Glass Company, Morgantown quickly developed a thriving glass industry. Seneca was the first glass factory in the city. The Morgantown Glass Works soon followed Seneca's example, opening for business in the city in 1899. By 1910, nine glass plants were located in the city. With the introduction of the glass industry to Morgantown, skilled glass artisans from France, Belgium, and Germany began arriving in significant numbers to fill positions in these firms.

Seneca Industrial District, no date (after 1910). *Courtesy of the Seneca Center and Riverfront Museums, Inc.*

Left to right: Morgantown Brick Works, Jones Window Glass Works, Seneca Glass Works, Morgantown Glass Works, 1902. *Courtesy of the Seneca Center and Riverfront Museums, Inc.*

As previously explained, most of the original managers for the Seneca Glass Company came from the Black Forest region of Germany. It is important to note that throughout most of the life of this company, management of the firm would remain in the hands of descendants of these original members. The firm's original stockholders were:

> Oto Jaeger, Ed Kammerer, Otto Sigwart, Andreas Koch, August Boehler, George Truog, Joseph A. Kammerer, and Leopold Sigwart. Otto Jaeger was president, Ed Kammerer, vice president, and George Truog, secretary-treasurer.

Not long afterwards, additional stockholders were brought into the firm, including:

> Frank Schmideger, Joseph Marshner, Joseph Stenger, A. Sigwart, A. Stenger, Peter and John Mellinger, A. Fontinelle, and William H. Bannister, Sr. and his brother Frank B. Bannister, who served alternately as company secretaries.
>
> (Robinson 1955, 94)

Examine the company records over the years and one quickly sees the same last names appearing again and again in one position or another.

1902 Seneca directors: many of the same families retained ownership throughout the company's history. *Courtesy of the Seneca Center and Riverfront Museums, Inc.*

The Seneca Glass Factory

Located in Morgantown's manufacturing district along the east bank of the Monongahela River, roughly one mile from the court house downtown, the Seneca factory was really a busy industrial complex with multiple buildings/shops, both large and small, interconnected by bridges, connecting doors, and corridors. At the center was the 80 x 80 foot blowing room, featuring a thirty-foot high (floor to ceiling), brick stack furnace, and 14 clay "pots" for melting batch into glass. The furnace itself measured over 30 feet in diameter and 9 feet high. This imposing structure was girdled with a metal ring containing hundreds of vents used to channel cool air directly to the glass blowers and their teams.

View of the furnace and blowing area, built in 1896. Photographed by Richard Sanders. *Courtesy of the Seneca Center and Riverfront Museums, Inc.*

The air compressor. Photographed by Richard Sanders. *Courtesy of the Seneca Center and Riverfront Museums, Inc.*

Overhead, the nineteenth-century wooden roof supports—a complex network of hundreds of supporting bridges, bolsters, girders, posts, rafters, and sills—were left exposed. Above them, louvered vents of a lantern were positioned high on the roof. These manually operated louvers could be opened to vent the heated air from the blowing room.

The original lehr room measured 60 x 60 feet, containing the tunnel-like annealing lehrs and the conveyor belt systems that passed glass through them. This room also featured a many louvered lantern in the roof. (Fleming Associates 1986)

In June 1902, a fire destroyed a large portion of the Seneca Glass factory, leaving behind much of the original 1896 brick construction encompassing the 14 pot furnace and the lehr. After the fire, insurance covered the reconstruction of the plant, directed by Elmer Jacobs, a prominent Morgantown architect known for his designs of Pittsburgh area glass factories, as well as local Morgantown commercial and residential structures.

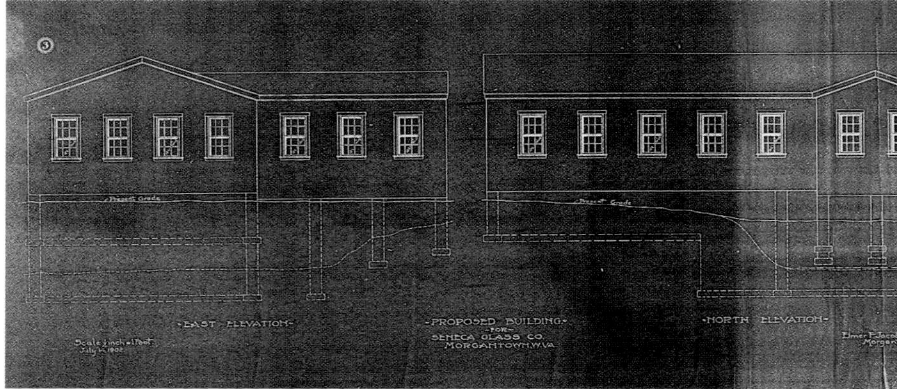

Elmer Jacobs blueprint of the 1902 Seneca addition. *Courtesy of the Seneca Center and Riverfront Museums, Inc.*

The devastation of the 1902 Seneca Glass Company fire. *Courtesy of the Seneca Center and Riverfront Museums, Inc.*

After reconstruction, as the years passed, the Seneca Glass Company would come to cover four acres of ground. Added to the central two-story structure were buildings housing cracking-off, smoothing, decorating, and packing departments, along with stock sheds, the loading department, a cooper's shop, and the company's main office building.

In 1913, Seneca built a second factory, Factory B, in nearby Star City, West Virginia. Factory B produced "lime blown," machine made tumblers and undecorated wares. Although shut down for almost a year in 1928-1929, Factory B would continue production into the 1930s. Included among Factory B's Depression era wares were a variety of colored glasswares including cobalt and transparent colors (such as light green and topaz) considered very modern in 1932. (McKenzie 1921; Delores 1986; Core 1982, 394; Core 1984, 35; Page et al. 1995, ix-x)

Town of Seneca

Following closely upon the heels of the construction of the original Seneca Glass factory in 1896, homes were quickly constructed near the factory to house its employees. The "Beechurst Addition" houses extended eastward, soon connecting with a development known then as Sunnyside. Within a year, the growing community had built a church and social hall. On February 5, 1898, the community voted to name the expanding town and its railway station "Seneca." Of this event, it was reported that

> the new town takes in a large scope of territory and will soon be a very important one. It has within its bounds the University and Morgantown proper can no longer be said to be the seat of that institution. (Core 1982, 227)

The claim to having West Virginia University within Seneca's boundaries was significant to its residents; a number of glass workers moved into the area to be near the University and send their children there when they were grown.

Seneca Glass Company script. Script was used instead of money to pay employees in the 1920s. *Courtesy of the Seneca Center and Riverfront Museums, Inc.*

Photograph of young boys working at Seneca Glass Company, 1902. Photograph donated to museum by Mr. Bernie Stenger. *Courtesy of the Seneca Center and Riverfront Museums, Inc.*

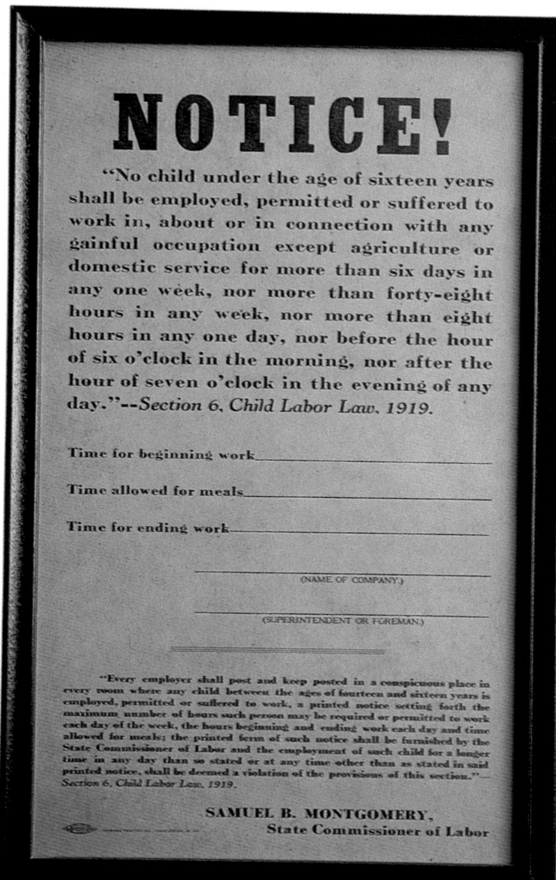

NOTICE!

"No child under the age of sixteen years shall be employed, permitted or suffered to work in, about or in connection with any gainful occupation except agriculture or domestic service for more than six days in any one week, nor more than forty-eight hours in any week, nor more than eight hours in any one day, nor before the hour of six o'clock in the morning, nor after the hour of seven o'clock in the evening of any day."--*Section 6, Child Labor Law, 1919.*

Time for beginning work__________

Time allowed for meals__________

Time for ending work__________

____
(NAME OF COMPANY.)

____
(SUPERINTENDENT OR FOREMAN.)

"Every employer shall post and keep posted in a conspicuous place in every room where any child between the ages of fourteen and sixteen years is employed, permitted or suffered to work, a printed notice setting forth the maximum number of hours such person may be required or permitted to work each day of the week, the hours beginning and ending work each day and time allowed for meals; the printed form of such notice shall be furnished by the State Commissioner of Labor and the employment of such child for a longer time in any day than so stated or at any time other than as stated in said printed notice, shall be deemed a violation of the provisions of this section."—*Section 6, Child Labor Law, 1919.*

SAMUEL B. MONTGOMERY,
State Commissioner of Labor

Child Labor law notice, circa 1919. *Courtesy of the Seneca Center and Riverfront Museums, Inc.*

Gathering of Seneca Glass Company employees, c. 1900s. *Courtesy of the Seneca Center and Riverfront Museums, Inc.*

Joseph Rancinger family: Joseph, Victor, Angeline, and Mary all worked for Seneca and other local glass firms. Photographed by R. DeAngelis. *Courtesy of the Seneca Center and Riverfront Museums, Inc.*

Seneca Production Through the Decades

Around 1920, the Seneca Glass Company would offer a new line of deep etched glassware. So numerous were the firm's offerings at this point that three catalogs were produced. The catalogs were divided by decorating techniques, one featuring light cut wares, another deep etched products, and the third contained a variety of "miscellaneous" wares. (Six 1991, 73)

Seneca Glass Co., 1920. *Courtesy of the Seneca Center and Riverfront Museums, Inc.*

In 1921, the company's officers were listed: Andrew Kammerer, president; Leopold Sigwart, vice president; and Charles F. Boehler, secretary and treasurer. Of the founding members, August Boehler, Leopold Sigwart, Otto Sigwart, and Andrew Kammerer remained active in the company. Charles Boehler was given much of the credit in the *Morgantown District Industrial and Business Survey* of 1921 for the company's success and productivity. The *Survey* stated that Seneca produced two to three car loads of lead blown bar and tableware every week. Mr. Boehler must have felt a bit like a victim of his own success, stating in 1921 that the factory was ready to expand its facilities, if only they could find the room!

Also by 1921, Seneca had established sample rooms around the country, another sign of the company's success. These were located in the main office in Morgantown, West Virginia, in New York City, Chicago, Illinois, Elberton, Georgia, and San Francisco, California. (McKenzie 1921)

Meanwhile, as previously stated, Seneca's Factory B in Star City, would turn out a wide variety of undecorated wares, tumblers, and colored glassware from 1913 on into the 1930s. The wares produced at Factory B would have been quite useful to the company as it entered into the Depression years (dating roughly from 1929 to the advent of World War II). During those lean years, expensive cut glass was overlooked in favor of less expensive wares of the type produced at Factory B.

In the mid-1930s, Robert Morrison, an experienced glass cutter, moved into the Seneca community with his wife Polly and their three children. In 1942, Morrison became Seneca's cutting manager. As cutting manager, he was in charge of a shop with thirty-one cutters. He oversaw both decorating and shipping. A close friend of his, Joe Buck, was then in charge of production on the plant's "hot" side, including overseeing the batch, pots, firing, and blowing. Between the two of them, Morrison and Buck coordinated the efforts of their respective charges and saw to the timely filling of orders. Robert Morrison remained

Original cutting room. *Courtesy of the Seneca Center and Riverfront Museums, Inc.*

Seneca Industrial District, circa 1921. *Courtesy of the Seneca Center and Riverfront Museums, Inc.*

with the company for forty-four years. During that time he oversaw the development of many of the firm's open stock patterns. It was reported that in 1984, some fifteen examples of Robert Morrison's Seneca crystal were in the care of the Cultural Center in Charleston, West Virginia. (Manning 1984, 44)

In 1947, Robert Morrison helped coordinate an upgrading of Seneca's original glass cutting machinery. The original machinery, including line shafts with wooden pulleys driven by a single motor, was housed in a 139-foot long room. Amazingly, that one motor powered every cutting lathe and polishing machine in the room. The system set one cutting speed for every cutting wheel, limiting the decorating possibilities. Also, vibrations in the line wasted many pieces and made fine cutting a difficult and time-consuming operation. In 1947, the company built a new addition featuring modern cutting equipment that increased the efficiency of the operation. (Fleming Associates 1986)

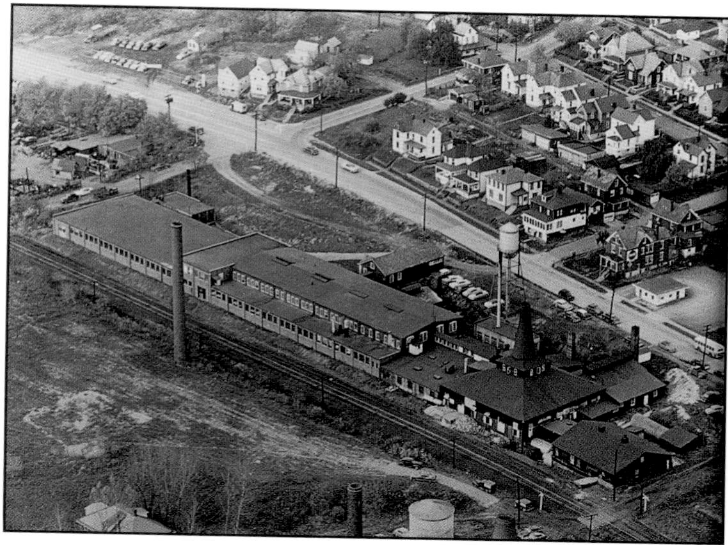

Aerial view of Seneca, showing the 1947 major addition, which housed the glass cutting department, circa 1960. *Courtesy of the Seneca Center and Riverfront Museums, Inc.*

Following the lean years of the Depression (lean for Americans, and Seneca—which was forced to close Factory B during the 1930s), elegant and expensive tablewares returned to favor. As the company entered the decade of the 1950s, however, it soon became apparent that the popularity of elegant glassware was to be short-lived. The Seneca Glass Company began producing less costly glassware more appropriate for informal dinners and parties—occasions which had been growing in favor and frequency with the American public since the Depression era.

Seneca's first offering in informal glassware was the Driftwood Casual series, a pattern that was to remain popular for nearly thirty years. Driftwood Casual, initially offered in limited forms and colors, was to be Seneca's best known product line in its time. As the years passed, new items, including beverage glasses, candy dishes, pitchers, and plates, in a wide variety of colors were added to the Driftwood Casual line. (Page et al. 1995, x-xi)

Rubber stamps, product identification stamps used to mark packing boxes. *Courtesy of the Seneca Center and Riverfront Museums, Inc.*

From company brochure, no date.

Patent drawing.

Seneca would enjoy the spotlight during the late 1950s and early 1960s. For three years running, 1956-1958, Seneca received the top award for fine quality tableware from B. Altman and Company of New York. Beginning on April 1, 1957, and continuing on throughout that summer, Seneca participated in the 350th anniversary celebration of the establishment of Jamestown, Virginia. Four other Morgantown glass firms joined Seneca in the festivities: Morgantown Glassware Guild, Beaumont Company, Davis-Lynch Glass Company, and Quality Glass Company. In the early 1960s, Seneca returned to the public's attention when they filled an order for Vice President Lyndon Johnson for Seneca glassware from the Epicure line. Mrs. Johnson placed the order and used the glassware, decorated with the Vice President's initials and a Stetson hat, in their home. Epicure was a tulip shaped stemware line featuring a delicate hand-drawn stem. Enjoying all this attention in the early 1960s were Seneca's president and treasurer Harry G. Kammerer, vice president Harry J. Sigwart, and secretary John W. Weimer. (Aull 1965, 6; Seneca Glass Company 1963)

From *Catalog No. R83*, pg. 10.

In 1973, Seneca again received public attention when the factory complex was added to the Historic American Engineering Records/West Virginia Survey. A documentary film about the factory was also produced at this time.

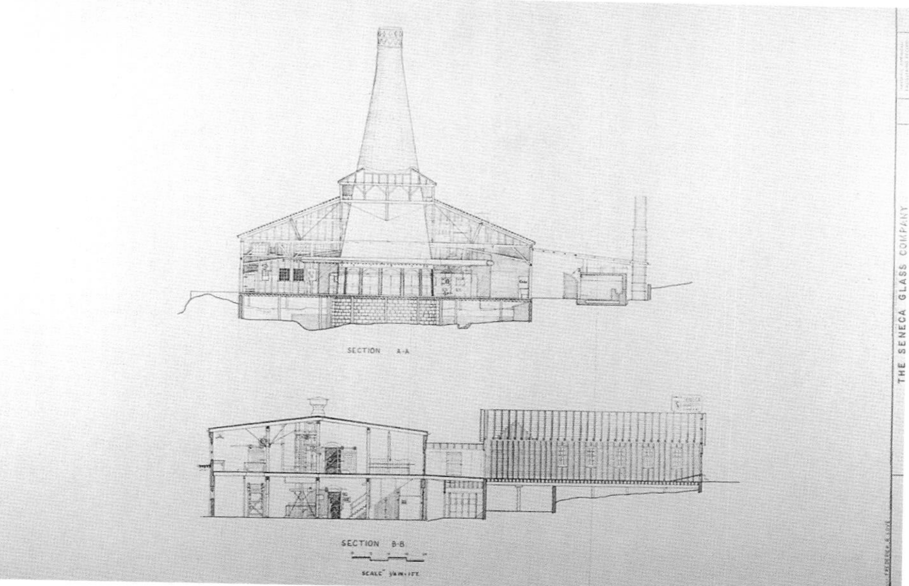

1973 Historic American Engineering Record cross-section drawing of the Seneca Glass Company complex. *Courtesy of the Seneca Center and Riverfront Museums, Inc.*

Trouble was afoot for Morgantown's glass companies in the 1970s. The *Morgantown Post* of April 8, 1971, reported that Morgantown's glass companies (Seneca Glass Company, Morgantown Glassware Guild, Gentile Glass Company, and Monongalia Valley Cut Glass Company among them) were threatened with collapse due to foreign competition.

In the face of their international competitors in the 1970s, Seneca produced a variety of informal glasswares in a number of eye-catching colors. Quite a few of these glassware lines would last no more than one or two years. Among the later wares produced by Seneca were pattern molded stemwares, covered candy bowls, stacking Christmas tree containers, and vases. Colors employed during the 1970s included Accent Red, Amber, Black, Buttercup, Cinnamon, Delphine Blue, Lime Green, Moss Green, Peacock Blue, Plum, Ritz Blue, and Sahara.

#50 The Tree, in accent red, drape optic, 10.75" h. $75-85.

#50A bowl (base of tree), in accent red, 4" h. $35-40.

Note: It is not always possible to find both the bases and tops of these trees together; over the years parts of items—bases, tops, stoppers, and lids, for example—may become broken or lost. However, collectors may choose to keep or purchases these pieces as representative pieces in a series, such as in this case, or in hopes of eventually finding the missing part.

#10 Evergreen Trees, two-part: in crystal, accent red, and moss green. 8.25" h. (overall); red example is missing the base. Complete trees: red, $50-60; crystal, $30-35; green, $35-40.

In 1982, the Seneca Glass Company was sold to a group of Malaysian investors. Now out of the hands of the descendants of the company's founders, the firm's name was changed to Seneca Crystal Incorporated. In August 1983, the company promptly filed for bankruptcy. The company's stock and equipment was then sold and dispersed. A sampling of Seneca's archival material today is conserved in the West Virginia University Regional History Collection.

In 1984, the Seneca building was purchased by Sanders Floor Covering Incorporated. In 1985, the Seneca factory was added to the National Register of Historic Places as a significant example of American history. Among the cited reasons for nomination were the structure and architecture of the buildings (as one might suspect), Seneca's role in the technology of glass making, the quality of Seneca's glassware and the skill of the laborers who produced it, and in recognition of the neighborhood that arose around the factory site. (Core 1984, 487; Page et al. 1995, x-xi; Fleming Associates 1986)

Since that time, the glass factory structure has been transformed through adaptive reuse into a complex of shops and a modest museum displaying many of the tools used to create Seneca's brilliant glassware, photographs of the original factory, its founders, and the surrounding town, and even preservation of the factory's original freight elevator. While many of the larger factory areas are now divided, much of the structure's original character remains, along with the massive furnace at the heart of the factory. Also of interest, the walls and corridors are decorated with paintings and murals dedicated to Seneca's past and the past of glassmaking. So, while Seneca no longer produces its varied glasswares that have so captured the attentions of today's collectors, the Seneca factory site may still be visited by all those who are interested in America's fascinating glassmaking past.

Freight elevator, made by the Marsall Brothers Company of Pittsburgh, Pennsylvania, installed 1902. Photographed by Richard Sanders. *Courtesy of the Seneca Center and Riverfront Museums, Inc.*

Seneca Factory Outlet & Gift Shop brochure, no date.

"Coca-Cola" bottle, made by Seneca Glass Company, Seneca etched on bottom, 2.5" h. $65-75.

Photograph of the original water tower for the Seneca plant, used today in many advertisements and promos for the museum. *Courtesy of the Seneca Center and Riverfront Museums, Inc.*

Paintings celebrating Seneca's rich glassmaking history adorn the walls and corridors of the former Seneca factory. This painting informally titled *Cheers* was painted from a 1940s photograph, which shows an unidentified group of members having a special celebration at a bar known (reportedly) as "The Hunting and Fishing Club." This club was (reportedly) located above Cappelantti's Grill on Walnut Street, in Morgantown, West Virginia. Some of the group were employees of Seneca Glass Company. (Note the gun case in the background.) Photograph: Unknown, Painted by Sally McLanin. *Courtesy of the Seneca Center and Riverfront Museums, Inc.*

Wares

~Ashtrays~

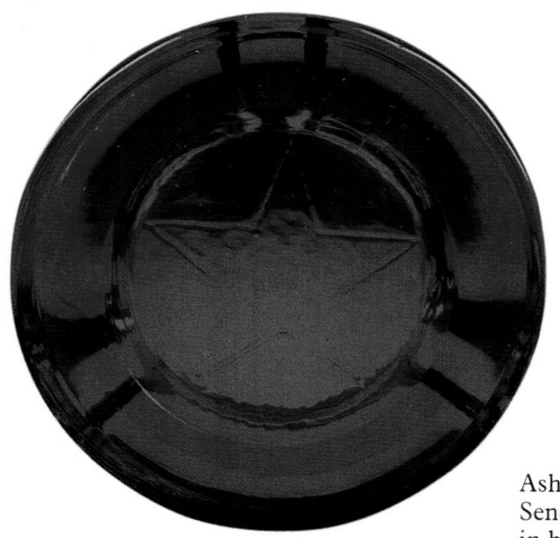

Ashtray with the Seneca Star impressed in bottom, in accent red, 3" dia. $50-60.

Ashtray, 0.75" h., 2.5" dia., and cigarette holder, 2.25" h. $125-140; $175-200.

~Bells~

Detail of bells, showing cut and handles.

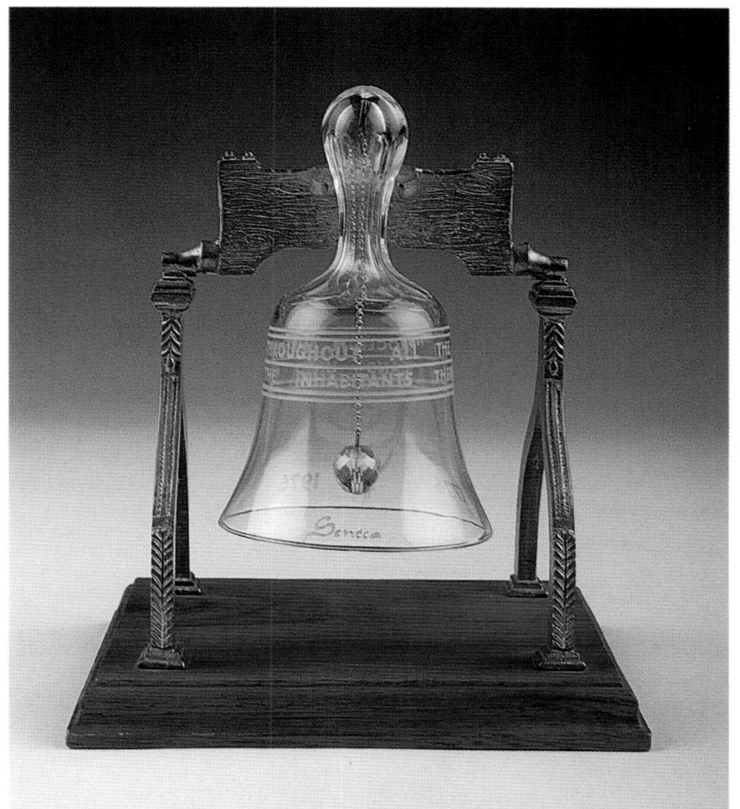

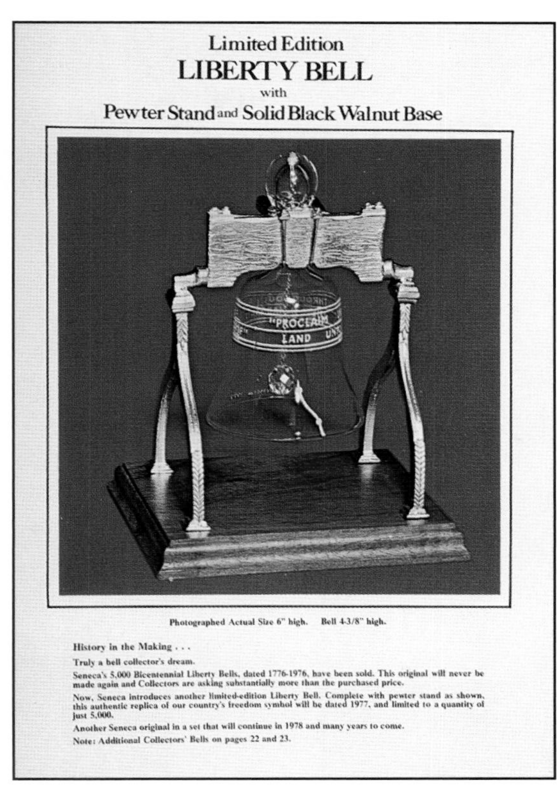

Limited Edition
LIBERTY BELL
with
Pewter Stand and Solid Black Walnut Base

Photographed Actual Size 6" high. Bell 4-3/8" high.

History in the Making . . .

Truly a bell collector's dream.

Seneca's 5,000 Bicentennial Liberty Bells, dated 1776-1976, have been sold. This original will never be made again and Collectors are asking substantially more than the purchased price.

Now, Seneca introduces another limited-edition Liberty Bell. Complete with pewter stand as shown, this authentic replica of our country's freedom symbol will be dated 1977, and limited to a quantity of just 5,000.

Another Seneca original in a set that will continue in 1978 and many years to come.

Note: Additional Collectors' Bells on pages 22 and 23.

Limited Edition Liberty Bell, 4.5" h. (bell only), with pewter stand and solid black walnut base. $45-55.

"History in the making . . . truly a bell collector's dream. Seneca's 5,000 Bicentennial Liberty Bells, dated 1776-1976, have been sold. This original will never be made again and collectors are asking substantially more than the purchased price.

Now, Seneca introduced another limited-edition Liberty Bell. Complete with pewter stand as shown, this authentic replica of our country's freedom symbol will be dated 1977, and limited to a quantity of just 5,000.

Another Seneca original in a set that will continue in 1978 and many years to come."

Seneca Glass Company, Catalogue no. 77

#1 bell, cut 1434 Heirloom pattern, 6.5" h. $50-60.

#2 bells: decoration unknown; cut 1318 Celeste pattern; cut 121 Laurel pattern; cut 1117 Solitare pattern. 3.75" h. $20-30 ea.

#3 bells: Regal; Reflection 3 optic; no cutting; moss green. 4.5" h. $25-35 ea.

#3 bells, cut 636 Stratford, 4.5" h. $25-35 ea.

#3 bells: Puritan; Chantilly; cut 848. 4.5" h. $25-35 ea. Primrose gold, $35-50.

#3 bells: West Virginia Centennial, 1863-1963; Monongalia County, West Virginia, Bicentennial, 1776-1976. 4.5" h. $25-35 ea.

#3 bells: cut 1452 Rosalynn pattern; cut 1448 Chalice pattern; cut 1318 Celeste pattern; cut 1426 Buckingham pattern. 4.5" h. $25-35 ea.

#3 bells: cut 1933; cut 1422 Orleans pattern; cut 1448 Chalice pattern; unknown cutting; cut 476 Windblown pattern. 4.5" h. $25-35 ea.

#3 bell and #4 bell in accent red. 4.375" h.; 5.5" h. $30-40; $40-55.

#3 bell, unidentified cut, rose etching, 4.25" h. NP.

#4 bells. *Left & 3rd from left:* cut 1447 Sunburst pattern; *2nd from left:* delphine blue; *right:* cut 121 Laurel pattern. 5.5" h. $35-50 ea.

#4 bells. *Left:* cut 1451 Brittany pattern; *middle two*: cut 1449 Tapestry pattern; *right:* unknown cutting. 5.5" h. $35-50 ea.

#4 bell, unidentified cut, floral etching, 5.5" h. NP.

#4 bell, unidentified cut, floral etching, 5.5" h. NP.

#4 bell (frosted), with holly berry, 5.5" h. $45-60.

#5 hanging bells, Christmas 1978 and Christmas 1979. 2.25" h. $15-20 ea.

#5 hanging bell, Christmas 1979, on wood stand, 4.5" h. (w/ stand). $15-20.

~Bottles/Carafes/Decanters~

Bottles

#6 bottle, 11" h., and No. 200 vase, 10.5" h. $20-25; $30-35.

Bottle or carafe, unidentified star cutting, 8" h. $40-50.

#6 bottle, 30 oz., unfinished from factory with marking lines, unidentified cut. $40-45.

Carafes

Carafe, cut 1436 Ardmore pattern, 6" h. $125-135.

Line 132, carafe, 32 oz., 9" h. $20-25.

Decanters

Decanter, no cut, 7.5" h. $25-30.

Decanter, unidentified cut, with cut stopper, 9.5" h. (w/o stopper). $125-140.

Detail of cutwork.

Decanter, Allegheny line, with black petal foot, with cut stopper, 10" h. (w/o stopper). $85-100.

Line 150, decanter, footed, cut 250, with cut stopper, 8.5" h. (w/o stopper); and tumbler, cut 250, 3.75" h. $15-20; decanter: $100-110.

Bowls

Finger, footed & grapefruit

Finger bowl, 2.5" h., 4.5" dia. $5-10.

Finger bowl, unidentified cut, 4" dia. $5-10.

Finger bowl, cut 1262 Ardis pattern, 4.5" dia. $10-15.

Finger bowl, footed, unidentified cut, 2.25" h. NP.

Finger bowl, footed, unidentified cut, 4.25" dia. $15-20.

Grapefruit bowl, footed, cut 250, 3" h. $20-30.

Finger bowl, footed, unidentified cut, 4.25" dia. $20-25.

Bowl, footed, cut 250, 5" h., 7.75" dia. $45-55.

Finger bowl, footed, cut 428, 2.25" h. $20-25.

Line 393, finger bowl, footed, unidentified cut, 3" h. $60-75.

Finger bowl, footed, cut 803, 2.5" h. NP.

Line 499, finger bowl, optic, cut 373, 2.125" h., 4.75" dia. NP.

Finger bowl, footed, cut 803, 4.125" dia. $15-20.

Line 616, finger bowl, cut 1078, 2.125" h., 4.5" dia. $15-20.

Line 1482, finger bowl, cut 987, 2.25" h., 4.75" dia. $35-45.

Line 1305, finger bowls, 4.25", 4.5", and 4.125" dia. $5-10 ea.

Line 1482, finger bowl, cut 583, 2.25" h., 5" dia. $20-30.

Line 1599, finger bowl, cut 801, 2.5" h. $15-20.

Line 1936, finger bowl, footed, cut 779, 2.5" h., 4.125" dia. $35-45.

Console

Console bowl, with four feet, unidentified cut, 12" dia. $90-110.

Rolled edge console bowl, unidentified cut, 3.5" h., 12" dia. $175-200.

Console bowl, cut 770, 12" dia. $120-130.

Line 180, console bowl, with six feet, cut 428, 3" h., 12.75" dia. $125-135.

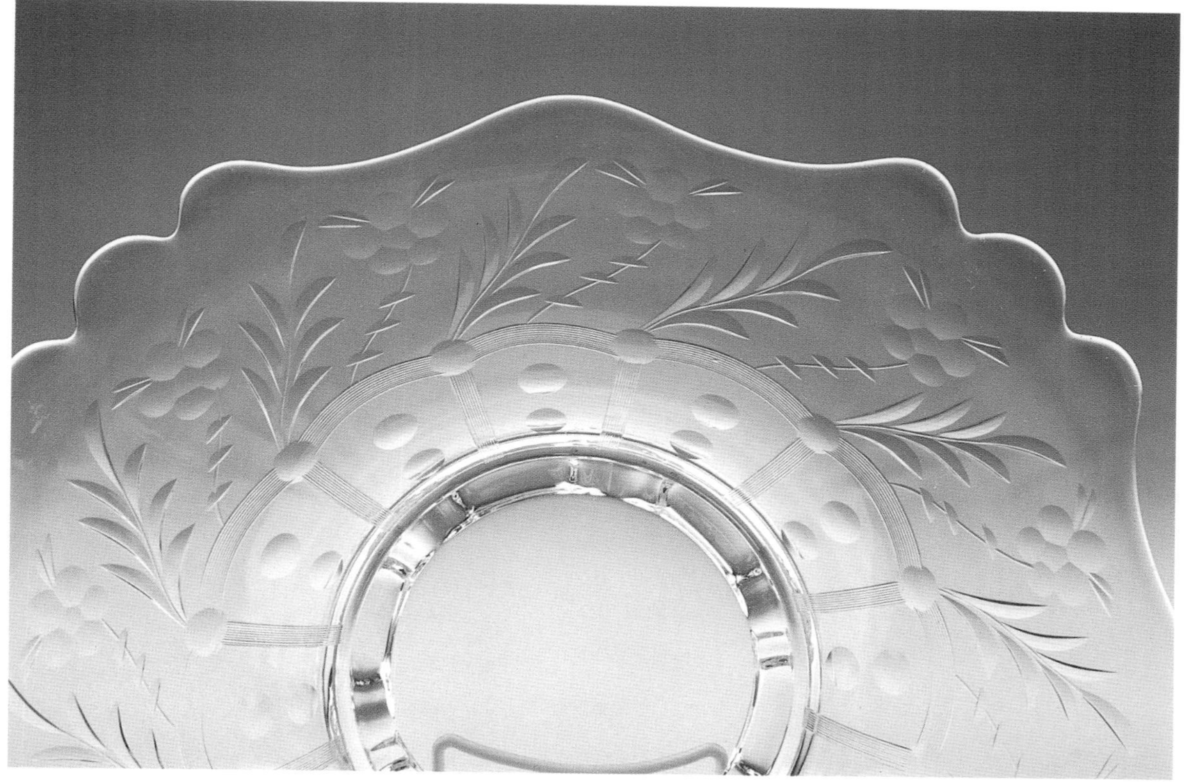

Detail of cutwork.

Below:
Line 499, rolled edge console bowl, cut 367, 11" dia. $125-150; and candlesticks, 3" h. $100-125 pr.

Line 515, console bowl, with six feet, unidentified cut, 13" dia. $90-110.

Detail of cut of console bowl.

Line 2503, console bowl, with three feet, cut 713, 12" dia. $90-110.

Detail of cut of console bowl.

~Candlesticks~

Rolled edge candlesticks, cut 476-2, 3" h., and marmalade jar, with lid, also cut 476-2, 3.25" h. $100-125 pr.; jar: $45-55 (w/o lid).

Rolled edge candlestick, cut 476-2, 3" h. $100-125 pr.

Line 176, rolled edge candlestick, rose lace etching, 3" h. $100-125 pr.

Detail of rose lace etching.

Line 1480, candlesticks (one turned to show cut foot), single light, scalloped square cut base, 4.75" h. NP.

Line 1480 candlesticks, two lights, cut foot, 5" h. $115-130 pr.

~Compotes~

Compote, unidentified cut, 7.25" h. $150-160.

Compote, unidentified cut, 7.25" h. $175-200.

Detail of top left compote.

Compote, unidentified cut, 6.75" h., 6.875" dia. $175-200.

Stem 150, compote, cut 250, 6.75" h. $140-155.

Stem 9936, compote, cut 1409, 5" h. $110-120.

~Cruets~

Cruet, unidentified cut, with cut stopper, 4.5" h. $50-60.

Cruet, "Seneca Glass Co., Morgantown, W. Va.," enameled, with cut stopper, 6" h. $75-85.

Cruet, without stopper, cut 121, 4.5 h. $50-60.

Cruet, with melon stopper, cut 4390, 4.5" h. $40-50.

~Custard Cups~

Custard cup, cut 1434, 2.125" h. $20-25.

Line 502, custard cup, cut 503, 2.25" h. $25-30.

~Ice Buckets~

Line 972, ice bucket or vase, cut 1448 Chalice pattern, 8". $100-125.

Line 1202, ice bucket and whiskey, cut 228. Bucket: 7.75" h. Whiskey: 2.75" h. $100-125 (bucket); $15-20.

~Jars~

Candy Jars

Covered candy jars by Seneca.

Covered candy jar, cut 460, 4" h. (w/o lid). $40-50.

Covered candy jar, cut 476-3, 9" h. (w/o lid). $65-75.

Covered candy jar, peacock optic, 7" h. (w/o lid). $45-50.

Covered candy jar, unidentified cut, 6.5" h. w/o lid. $75-80.

Covered candy jar, unidentified multiple cuts on bowl, lid, and foot, 6.5" h. (w/o lid). $250-300.

#455 covered candy, unidentified cut, with black foot and lid, 6" h. (w/o lid). $80-95.

Covered candy jar, unidentified cut, with black foot, 6.25" h. (w/o lid). $95-110.

Eggs

#1 egg, unidentified cut, with black lid, 5" h. (w/o lid). $45-60.

Ginger Jars

Covered ginger jar, no cut, 6.5" h. (w/o lid). $45-50.

#80 ginger jar, unidentified cut, 4.75" h. (w/o lid). $110-125.

#80 ginger jar, cut 958 Harvest pattern, with original label, 4.75" h. (w/o lid). $135-150.

#90 ginger jar, unidentified cut, 4.75" h. (w/o lid). $110-125.

#80 ginger jar, cut 1457 Lovebirds pattern, 4.75" h. (w/o lid). $110-125.

#90 ginger jar, cut 960 Butterfly pattern, 4.75" h. (w/o lid). $110-125.

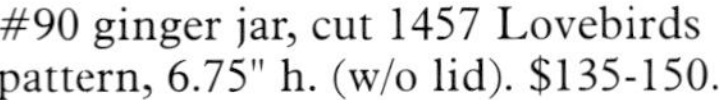

#90 ginger jar, cut 1457 Lovebirds pattern, 6.75" h. (w/o lid). $135-150.

#90 ginger jar, cut 960 Butterfly pattern, 8.5" h. (w/ lid). $135-150.

#90 ginger jar, cut 1457 Lovebirds pattern, 8.5" h. (w/o lid). $135-150.

Marmalade Jars

Covered marmalade jar, unidentified cut, 3" h. (to rim). $25-30.

Covered marmalade, unidentified cut, 3.75" h. (to rim). $45-55.

~Lemonades~

Line 150, lemonades, handled, cut 250, 5.5" h. $25-30.

~Parfaits~

#11 parfait, in crystal, 6" h. $10-15.

~Pitchers~

Pitchers & Tankards

Pitcher, unidentified cut, 7.5" h. $40-50.

Pitcher, monogrammed "W," 9.75" h. $60-75.

Pitcher, unidentified cut, 9" h. $60-75.

Pitcher, 9.25" h., and tumbler, 4" h., cut 476-13. $75-85; $15-20.

Tankard, unidentified cut, 8.5" h. $45-55.

Tankard, unidentified cut, 8.5" h. $60-75.

Tankard, 8.5" h., and finger bowl, 4.5" dia., unidentified cut. $50-60; $20-25.

Tankard, cut 360, 1/2-pint, 4.5" h. $60-75.

Tankard, cut 360, 8.5" h. $60-75.

Tankard, cut 560, 3-pint, 9.25" h. $70-80.

Line 476, tankard, cut 1074 and 43, Spray pattern, 9" h. $50-60.

~Plates~

Handled sandwich plate, 10" dia. (not including handles), and creamer and sugar, 3.5" h., unidentified cut. Plate: $125-140; sugar & creamer: $125-150 set.

Plate, unidentified cut, 7.5" dia. $15-20.

Plate, unidentified cut, 8.25" dia. $15-20.

Three-part relish, unidentified cut, 8.25" dia. $120-135.

Plate, cut 121 Laurel pattern, 6.5" dia. $10-15.

Plate, cut 287, 8.25" dia. $15-20.

Plate, cut 287, 8.5" dia. $15-20.

Plate, cut 671 Greenbrair pattern, 8.5" dia. $20-25.

Line 190, set of plates, cut 190-4, 8.5" dia. $25-30 ea.

Line 499, plate, cut 367, 8.5" dia. $20-25.

Line 908, plate, cut 859 Renaissance pattern, 8.5" dia. $15-20.

Line 916, plates, unidentified cut, 8" dia. $25-35.

Detail of plate.

Line 916, two plates, 8.5" and 8" dia., and finger bowl, cut 916-1, 4.5" dia. $30-40.

Line 1482, handled sandwich salver, cut 442 Thistle pattern, 10.25" sq. $125-140.

Line 1934, plates, cut 777 Windsor pattern, 8.5" dia. $35-45.

Detail of plate.

Line 1965, plate, cut 1421 Anniversary pattern, 7.5" dia. $20-25.

Line 4816, plates, cut 4816-1, 8.5" and 8" dia. $35-45.

~Punch Bowls~

Punch bowl, footed, with 12 punch cups. Extremely nice, yet unidentified, cut. Bowl, 8.875" h., 10" dia.; cup, 2.25" h. Bowl, $3500; cups, $55-65 ea.

~Salts~

Individual salts, unidentified cuts, 1" h., 2.5" dia. $25-35 ea.

~Saucer Sherbets~

Saucer sherbet, footed, cut 1275. Saucer: 5.625" dia.; sherbet: 2.5" h. $45-55.

~Series~

Artichoke series, line 1985, in accent red: beverage, 5" h., and goblet, 6.375" h. $10-15; $20-25.

Artichoke series, line 1985: goblet, hi-ball and footed juice/wine in charm blue ranging in height from 3.75" to 6.375" h. On the Rocks in crystal and delphine blue, 3.25" h. Goblet: $10-15; others: $5-10 ea.

Baubles series, stem 1025: white wine, 5.25" h.; water goblet, 6.5" h.; red wine, 5.75" h. $10-15 ea.

Brocado series, juice/wine, footed, in morocco (brown), 4.25" h. $5-10.

Cascade series, line 1972, cocktail juice and tumbler in crystal, 3.25" h. and 6.75" h. $5-10 ea.

Cabaret series, line 1964, wine, 9 oz., in crystal, 5.625" h. $5-10.

Cascade series, line 1972, bowl, in brown, 2.25" h. $5-10.

Cascade series, line 1972, beverage and bar pitcher in peacock blue: pitcher, 40 oz., 10" h.; beverage, 15-1/2 oz., 5.25" h. Pitcher: $35-45; beverage: $8-12.

Cascade series, line 1972: beverage, 15-1/2 oz., 5.25" h.; cocktail/juice, 3.75" h.; Old Fashion, 11-1/2 oz., 3.75" h.; bar pitcher, 40 oz., with crystal stir rod and handle, 10.5" h.; footed juice/wine, 9 oz., 4.375" h. All in accent red. Pitcher: $45-60; ftd. juice/wine: $15-20; others: $12-15.

Driftwood Casual series label.

Original Driftwood Casual series, in assorted pastel colors with "Driftwood" designed on side. The original Driftwood was designed in 1953. Tumblers, 3.75" to 5.75" h. $15-20 ea.

Detail of pattern of Driftwood Casual series.

Other glass companies produced glassware similar in pattern to the Driftwood Casual series by Seneca. *Left,* in Delphine blue by Seneca. *Center,* Crinkle series by Morgantown Glassware Guild. *Right,* unknown.

Driftwood Casual series, in crystal: iced tea, 16 oz., 5.75" h.; roly poly, footed; pitcher, 65 oz., 10" h.; parfait, 7 oz., 5" h.; covered candy jar, footed, 4" h., 4.5 dia. Pitcher: $75-80; candy: $40-50; roly poly: $12-18; others: $10-15.

Driftwood Casual series, in heather: pitcher, 56 oz., 10" h., and 32 oz., 8" h.; iced tea, 16 oz., 5.75" h.; juice, 6 oz., 4.25" h.; roly poly, 12 oz., 3.375" h.; flowerlite, 5" dia.; cocktail, 6 oz., 3.375" h. Pitchers: $75-85 & $55-65; flowerlite: $20-25; others: $10-15.

Driftwood Casual series, in peacock blue: pitchers, 32 oz., and 65 oz.; covered candy jar, 4" h.; flowerlite, 3.5" h., 5" dia.; roly poly, 12 oz., 3.375" h.; bud vase, 7.25" h. Pitchers: $55-65 & $75-80; candy: $40-50; flowerlite: $20-25; roly poly: $10-15; vase: $15-20.

Driftwood Casual series, in peacock blue: single Old Fashion, 9 oz., 3.25" h.; double Old Fashion, 14 oz., 3.75" h.; hi-ball, 12 oz., 5.125" h.; iced tea, 16 oz., 5.75" h.; handled iced tea or beer mug, 16 oz., 5.75" h. Mug/iced tea: $20-25; others: $10-15.

Driftwood Casual series, in charm blue: pitcher, 65 oz., 10" h.; bud vase, 7.25" h.; goblet, footed, 13 oz., 5.5" h.; beverage cooler, 20 oz., 6.75" h.; juice, 6 oz., 4.25" h.; double Old Fashion, 14 oz., 3.75" h. Pitcher: $75-80; others: $15-20.

Driftwood Casual series, in delphine blue: pitchers, 32 oz., 8" h., and 65 oz., 10" h.; beer mug or handled iced tea, 16 oz., 5.75" h. Pitchers: $55-65 & $75-80; mug/ iced tea: $20-25.

Driftwood Casual series, in cobalt: double Old Fashion, 14 oz., 3.75" h.; grapefruit, 3.25" h.; roly poly, 12 oz., 3.375" h.; salad plate, 8.5" dia.; iced tea, 16 oz., 5.75" h.; beverage cooler, 20 oz., 7" h.; sherbet, 3.75" dia., 3" h. Grapefruit: $25-30; others: $20-25.

Plate from series, in cobalt. $20-25.

Driftwood Casual series, ashtrays, in cobalt blue, amber, and buttercup. 6" dia. $10-15.

Driftwood Casual series, in buttercup: hi-ball, 12 oz., 5.125" h.; goblet, footed, 13 oz., 5.5" h.; iced tea, 16 oz., 5.75" h.; roly poly, footed, 12 oz., 4" dia.; sherbet, 3" h., 3.75" dia.; pitchers, 32 oz., 8" h., and 65 oz., 10" h. Pitchers: $55-65 & $75-80; goblet: $12-18; others: $10-15.

Driftwood Casual series, in amber: covered candy jar, 4" h. (w/o lid); flowerlite, 5" dia.; goblet, footed, 13 oz., 5.5" h.; parfait, 7 oz., 5" h.; flower vase, 6.5" h.; goblet (frosted), 13 oz., 5.5" h. NP.

Driftwood Casual series, in amber: Old Fashion, 9 oz., 3.5" h.; double Old Fashion, 14 oz., 3.75" h.; juice, 6 oz., 4.25" h.; hi-ball, 12 oz., 5.125" h.; iced tea, 16 oz., 5.75" h. $10-15 ea.

Driftwood Casual series, in amber and moss green, salad or fruit bowls, 5" h., 9" dia. $45-55 ea.

Driftwood Casual series, in moss green: beer mug or handled iced tea, 16 oz., 5.75" h.; water goblet, stemmed, 6.25" h.; juice, 6 oz., 4.25" h.; pitchers, 32 oz., 8" h., and 65 oz., 10" h. Pitchers: $55-65 & $75-80; mug/iced tea: $20-25; others: $10-15.

Driftwood Casual series, in green: pitcher, 65 oz., 10" h.; beverage cooler, 20 oz., 7" h.; goblet, footed, 13 oz., 5.5" h. Pitcher: $75-80; others: $15-20.

Driftwood Casual series, in amethyst: 65 oz. pitcher; 37 oz. pitcher; 16 oz. iced tea. $75-80; $55-65; $10-15.

Driftwood Casual series, in accent red, pitcher, with crystal handle, 65 oz., 10" h. $90-110.

Driftwood Casual series, in brown, pitcher, 32 oz., 8" h. $55-65.

Driftwood Casual series, in cinnamon, pitchers, 32 oz., 8" h., and 65 oz., 10" h. $55-65; $75-80.

Driftwood Casual series, in charcoal, hollow stem beer glass, 5.5" h., and salad or fruit bowl, 5" h., 9" dia. $20-25; $45-55.

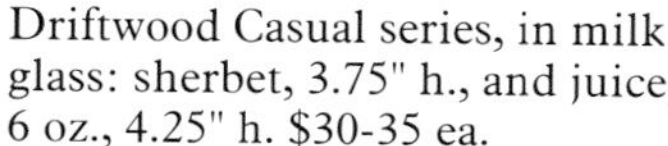

Driftwood Casual series, in milk glass: sherbet, 3.75" h., and juice, 6 oz., 4.25" h. $30-35 ea.

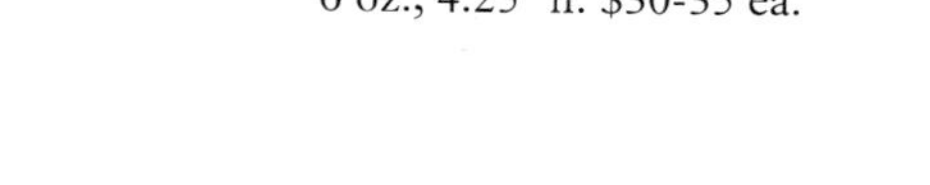

Driftwood Casual series pitchers, showing twelve of the fourteen colors, 65 oz. and 32 oz.

The Fashionables series, line 1974, in assorted colors: high stem dessert, in evergreen, 4.75" h.; low stem juice/wine, in moss green, 3.5" h.; Old Fashion, in brown, 4" h.; high stem juice/wine, in delphine blue and charm blue, 5.25" h. $5-10 ea.

The Fashionables, line 1974, in yellow: high goblet, 6.25" h.; low goblet, 4.25" h.; tall sherbet or high stem dessert, 4.5" h.; high stem juice/wine, 5.25" h.; Old Fashion, 4" h. $5-10 ea.

The Fashionables series, line 1974, in yellow, low stem juice/wine, 3.5" h. $5-10.

The Fashionables series, line 1974, in royal: footed juice/wine tumbler, and On the Rocks. 3.5" h. $10-15 ea.

The Fashionables series, in black: water goblet, 7.25" h.; iced tea, 6.75" h.; cocktail, 5.25" h.; champagne, 6" h.; low stem juice/wine, 3.25" h.; high stem sherbet, 6.25" h. Goblet & iced tea: $15-20; others: $10-20.

The Fashionables series, line 1974, low desserts, 3" h., in accent red, crystal, and royal blue. $20-25; $10-15; $20-25.

Company brochure, no date.

The Fashionables series, line 1974, mixers, in brown and moss green, 10.5" h. $35-40.

Gourmet Collection series, line 5321, vintage wine goblets, 14 oz., 7" h. $15-20.

Gourmet Collection series, dessert champagne with an etched shield on the bowl, 5.25" h. $15-20.

Gourmet Collection series, line 5321, Connoisseur line: vintage wine goblet, 7" h.; tulip champagne, 8" h.; brandy, 4.5" h.; sherry, 6" h. $15-20.

Images series, in crystal: wine, footed, 5" h., and hi-ball, 5.25" h. $5-10 ea.

Detail to show Seneca etched in base. Signature on bottom.

Le Chateau series.

Le Chateau series, line 1977, cabinet wine, cut 121, 9" h. $20-25.

Quilt series, in charm blue, tumbler, 4.5" h. $5-10.

Sculpture series, in lime green: double Old Fashion, 3.75" h., and goblet, footed, 5.25" h. $5-10 ea.

Socialables series, line 3875, in green: juice/cocktail, 9 oz., 3.25" h., and beverage, 16 oz., 5.125" h. $5-10 ea.

Seville series, line 1978, goblets, in crystal, green (with crystal foot), and yellow, 7" h. $5-10 ea.

~Shakers~

Shaker set, cut 476-3: martini mixer, with metal lid (manufacturer unknown), 9.25" h. (w/o lid); ice bucket, 5" h.; tumbler, 5.5" h. Mixer: $35-40; bucket: $20-25; tumbler: $5-10.

~Slim Jims~

Slim Jims, in assorted colors, ranging in size from 4" to 8.75" h. $25-30 ea.

Slim Jim, Pilsner type in amber, 8.25" h. $30-35

Stem 903, in amethyst, royal, amber, and forest green, with square feet, 8.625" h. $25-30 ea.

Wine, 7" h., and water goblet, 8.125" h., unidentified cut. $30-35.

~Stems~

Pair of cordials, 3.25" h. $15-20 ea.

Wine, 5.125" h. $15-20.

Iced tea, unidentified cut, 6.5" h. $30-35.

Water goblet, unidentified cut, 8.75" h. $60-70.

Low cocktail, unidentified cut, 3.5" h. $25-30.

Brandy snifter, unidentified cut, 6.25" h. $40-50.

Hollow stem wine, unidentified cut, 5.5" h. $30-35.

Hollow stem wine, unidentified cut, 5.25" h. $50-60.

Hollow stem wine, unidentified cut. 5.25" h. $35-45.

Cocktail, with nude, frosted stem, evergreen bowl, 6" h. $150.

Detail of stem.

Three wines, in evergreen, accent red, and amber bowls, with nude figural stems, 6" h. $150 ea.

High grapefruit bowl, cut 250, 5.75" h. $10-15.

Hollow stem wine, cut 839-1/2, 5.25" h. $25-30.

Tumbler, stemmed and footed, cut 1453 Majestic pattern, 5" h. $35-40.

Stem 7, peach champagne, cut 43, 19 oz., 12" h. Made when the West Virginia University Mountaineers played in the Peach Bowl, circa 1969. $50-60.

Sherbet, deep etch 609 Rose design, 3.25" h. $10-15.

Cordial, with cobalt foot and silver/chrome band, 5.25" h. $15-20.

Stem 9, cordial and brandy, both made for Harrah's casino in Reno, Nevada, dating from 1975. 4.75" h. $15-20 ea.

Stem 56, cut 1336 Florentine pattern: iced tea, 6.5" h.; water goblet, 5" h.; champagne, 4.25" h.; wine, 4.25" h.; cordial, 3.5" h. $8-12.

Stem 56, water goblet, cut 636 Stratford pattern, 6.75" h. $20-30.

Stem 56, cut 1343: water goblet, 6" h.; champagne, 4.5" h.; juice, 4.875" h.; sherry, 4" h.; cocktail, [illegible]875" h.; cordial, 3.25" h. $15-20 ea.

Stem 77 (twisted): iced tea, 7.25" h.; water goblet, 7" h.; champagne, 4.75" h.; saucer champagne, 6.25" h.; cocktail, 5" h.; wine, 5.75" h.; cordial, 3.75" h. $10-15 ea.

Below:
Stem 77 (twisted): wine, 5.75" and 6.125" h.; cocktail, 4" h; brandy, 4.75" h. $10-15 ea.

Stem 77, water goblet, cut 77-1, 7.5" h. $35-45.

Stem 128, water goblet, cut 1330-1/2, 6.25" h. $15-20.

Stem 150, hollow stem wine, cut 250, 5" h. $30-35.

Stem 155: goblet, 6.75" h.; champagne, 5.5" h.; claret, 5.5" h.; wine, 4.5" h.; cordial, 4" h.; sherry, 5.125" h. $15-20 ea.

Assortment of stem 156 and stem 155, showing differences in the stems. $15-20 ea.

Stem 152, brandy, cut 692-1/2, 5" h. $25-35.

Stem 152, cordial, cut 796, 4.125" h. $25-30.

Stem 164, wine, cut 164-1, with bubble in stem, 5.75" h. $20-30.

Stem 156, goblet, 6.5" h. $15-20.

Stem 164, pair of water goblets, cut 164-1, 7" h. $25-30 ea.

Stem 164, wine, cut 803, 5.75" h. $20-25.

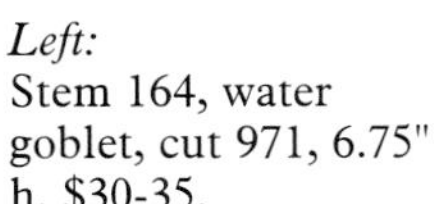

Left:
Stem 164, water goblet, cut 971, 6.75" h. $30-35.

Right:
Stem 164, water goblet, cut 980, 7" h. $30-35.

Left:
Stem 164, hollow stem wine, cut 971, 6" h. $75-90.

Right:
Stem 164, water goblet, cut 1120 Maytime pattern, 7" h. $35-40.

Stem 164, wines, cut 1121 Classic pattern, 5.25" h. $25-30.

Stem 180, wine, cut 476-3, 5.25" h. $10-15.

Stem 180, cut 428: water goblet, 8" h. $30-35; champagne, 5.5" h. $25-30; parfait, 6.25" h. $25-30; cocktail, 5.5" h. $25-30; wine, 6.25" h. $25-30.

Stem 180, cut 692-1/2: iced tea, 6" h.; parfait, 6.25" h.; tall champagne, 6.25" h.; champagne, 6.25" h.; juice, 5.75" h.; cordial, 4.5" h.; red wine, 6" h.; white wine 5.875" h.; cocktail, 5.75" h.; sherry, 5.25" h.; claret, 4.75" h. $20-25 ea.

Stem 190, water goblets, cut 190-2, with cut feet, 8" h. $50-60.

Stem 190, hollow stem honeycomb cut champagne, cut 190-7, 5.25" h. $35-50.

Detail of hollow stem honeycomb cut champagne.

Stem 190, wine, cut 190-7, 5.875" h. $25-30.

Stem 190, water goblet, cut 453, 8" h. $25-30.

Stem 190, cut 720: water goblet, 8" h.; iced tea, 7" h.; champagne, 5.75" h.; sherbet, 5.75" h.; cocktail, 5" h.; red wine, 6" h.; white wine, 5.75" h.; sherry, 5.125" h.; juice, 5.5" h. $15-20 ea.

Stem 256 (twisted), cocktail, cut 1356, 5.5" h. $15-20.

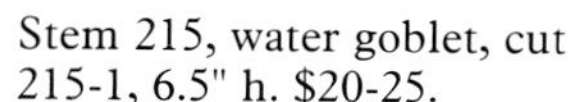

Stem 215, water goblet, cut 215-1, 6.5" h. $20-25.

Stem 256 (twisted), water goblet, cut 1357. $8-12.

Stem 215, water goblet, cut 636, 6.25" h. $25-30.

Assortment of stem 256 (twisted), cut 1432: iced tea, 6.75" h.; water goblet, 7" h.; cordial, 3.25" h.; champagne, 4.25" h.; cocktail, 4.25" h.; wine, 5.25" h.; sherry, 5.125" h. $15-20 ea.

Stem 260, cut 774: water goblet, 7.25" h.; champagne, 5.5" h.; low champagne, 4.5" h.; cocktail, 4.5" h.; juice, 5.75" h.; brandy, 5.25" h.; cordial, 4" h. $15-20 ea.

Stem 307, water goblet, unidentified cut, 6" h. *Courtesy of Steve and Anna Britvec.* $15-20.

Stem 310, water goblet, amber, no cut, 6" h. $20-25.

Set of four cordials, ranging in size from 3" to 3.5" h. *Left to right:* stem 310 with moss green stem; stem 520 with a crystal bowl and milk glass stem and foot; stem 526, cut 1219; stem 526, unidentified bowl. $25-30 ea.

Stem 331-1 (taller than 331), wine, cut 796, 6.25" h. $20-25.

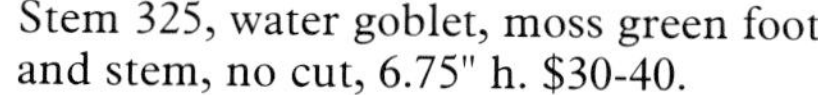

Stem 325, water goblet, moss green foot and stem, no cut, 6.75" h. $30-40.

Stem 325, low wines, with pressed stem, moss foot and stem, 3.5" h. $20-30.

Detail of paper label.

Stem 352, water goblet, cut 803, with bubble in stem, 7.25" h. $20-25.

Stem 352, water goblet, cut 1229 Caprice pattern, 7" h. $25-35.

Assortment of stem 352, cut 1252: iced tea, 7.25" h.; champagne, 5.25" h.; cocktail, 4.125" h.; cordial, 4" h.; sherry, 5" h.; wine, 5.25" h.; claret, 5.625" h. $20-25 ea.

Stem 352, cut 1262 Ardis pattern: water goblet, 7.25" h. $25-35; champagne, 5.5" h. $20-30; wine sherbet, 5" h. $20-30.

Stem 355, water goblet, cut unknown, 6.5" h. $15-20.

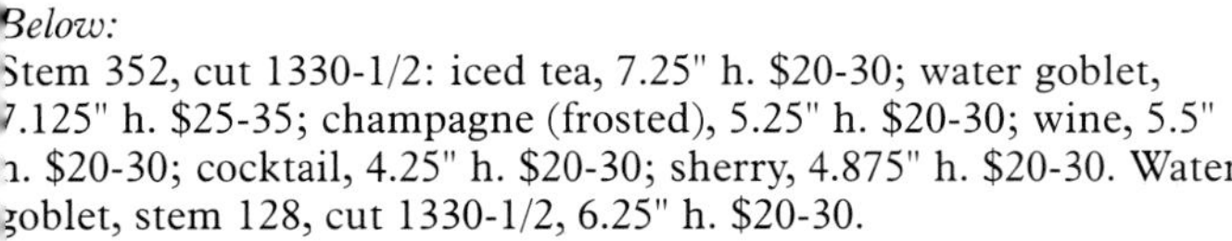

Below:
Stem 352, cut 1330-1/2: iced tea, 7.25" h. $20-30; water goblet, 7.125" h. $25-35; champagne (frosted), 5.25" h. $20-30; wine, 5.5" h. $20-30; cocktail, 4.25" h. $20-30; sherry, 4.875" h. $20-30. Water goblet, stem 128, cut 1330-1/2, 6.25" h. $20-30.

Stem 355, wine, cut 1375, 5.25" h. $10-15.

Stem 459, water goblet, black amethyst foot, 5.25" h. $10-15.

Stem 459: decoration 401, in yellow, 6" h.; decoration 401, in red, 5.5" h.; decoration 400, in blue, 5.5" h.; decoration 402, in red, 5" h.; decoration 388, red, 4.5" h. Goblet, stem 470, decoration 494, red, 7" h. $20-25 ea.

Stem 470, water goblet, cut 868, 7.25" h. $30-35.

Stem 475, water goblet, cut 258, 7.5" h. $40-50.

Stem 470, iced teas with jeweled stem, cut 868, 7.5" h. $45-55.

Stem 475, water goblet, cut 441, 7.25" h. $30-35.

Stem 476, water goblet, cut 476-2, 8.25" h. $25-35.

Stem 475, cut 832: champagne, 4.75" h.; parfait, 6" h.; cocktail, 4.75" h.; cordial, 3.75" h. $10-15 ea.

Stem 476, water goblet, cut 476-4, 8.25" h. $25-35.

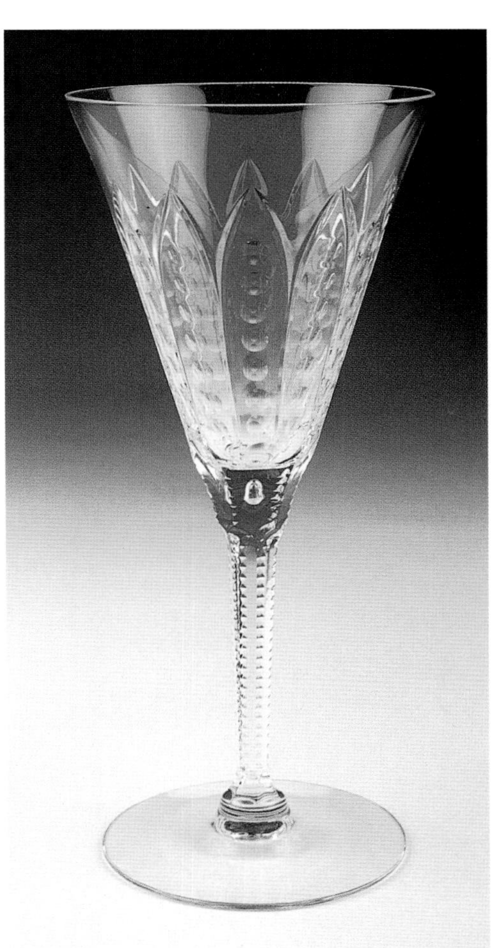

Stem 476, water goblet, cut 476-10, 8.5" h. $25-35.

Stem 476, water goblet, cut 476-11, 8.25" h. $25-35.

Stem 476, water goblet, cut 476-12, 8.25" h. $25-35.

Stem 476, water goblet, cut 627 Rhythm pattern, 8.25" h. $25-35.

Stem 476, water goblet, cut 636 Stratford pattern, 8.25" h. $25-35.

Stem 476, assortment of stemware, cut 636 Stratford pattern: water goblet, 8.5" h. $25-35; tall champagne, 6.5" h. $20-30; low champagne or sherbet, 5.25" h. $20-30; cordial, 4.5" h. $25-35; red wine, 6" h. $20-30; cocktail, 5.5" h. $20-30; juice tumbler, 3.5" h. $20-30; bell, 4.5" h. $20-30.

Left:
Stem 476, water goblet, cut 671 Greenbriar pattern, 8.5" h. $20-35.

Right:
Stem 476, water goblet, cut 682, 8.5" h. $25-35.

Stem 476, water goblet, cut 770 Gothic pattern, 8.25" h. $25-35.

Stem 476, water goblet, cut 726, 8.25" h. $25-35.

Stem 476, cut 770 Gothic pattern: water goblet, 8.25" h., $25-35, and wine, 6" h., $20-30.

Assortment of stem 476, cut 796: champagne, 6.5" h. $20-30; cordial, 5" h. $20-30; juice, 5.75" h. $20-30; tall wine, 6" h. $20-30; cocktail (frosted), 5" h. $20-30; sherry, 6" h. $20-30; low wine, 5.25" h. $20-30; finger bowl, 4.5" dia. $15-20; tumbler, 5.25" h. $15-20; juice, 4" h. $15-20.

Stem 476, water goblet, cut 846, 8.25" h. $25-35.

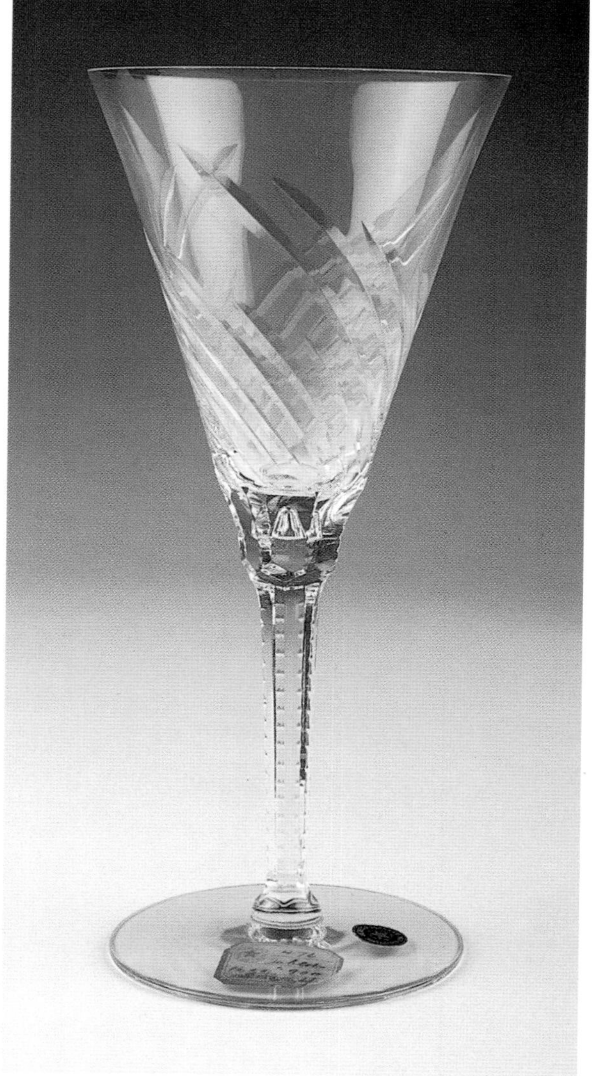

Stem 476, water goblet, cut 900 Windblown pattern, 8.25" h. $25-35.

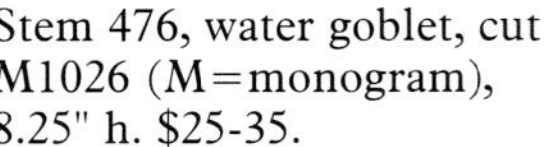
Stem 476, water goblet, cut M1026 (M=monogram), 8.25" h. $25-35.

Stem 476, water goblet, cut 967 Elegance pattern, 8.25" h. $25-35.

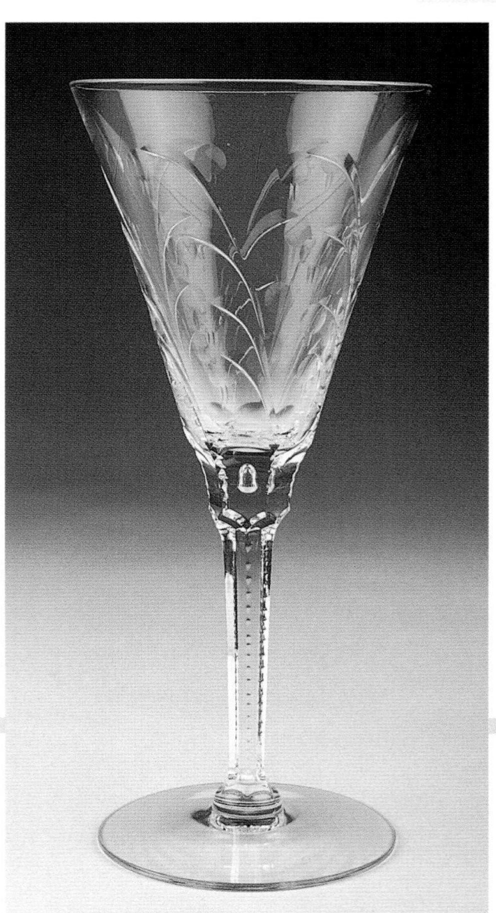

Stem 476, water goblet, cut 1073 Moderne pattern, 8.25" h. $25-35.

Stem 484, cordial, unidentified cut, 4.625" h. $25-30.

Stem 484, water goblet, unidentified cut, 8.25" h. $35-45.

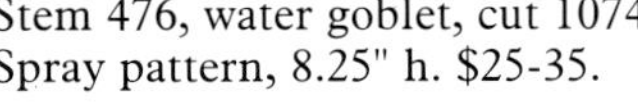

Stem 476, water goblet, cut 1074 Spray pattern, 8.25" h. $25-35.

Stem 484, cut 369: iced tea, 7" h.; cocktail, 5" h.; wine, 6" h.; juice, 4.75" h.; cordial, 4.5" h. NP.

Stem 485, sherry, unidentified cut, 5.5" h. $20-25.

Stem 484, water goblet, etch Sang Bleu, 8.25" h. $40-50.

Stem 492, wine, cut 287, 4.5" h. $15-20.

Stem 492, champagne, cut 299, 6.25" h. $25-30.

Stem 515, water goblet, no cut (monogrammed), 8" h. $15-20.

Stem 515, water goblet, no cut, 8" h. $15-20.

Assortment of stem 516, cut 1041, with square foot: claret, 5.5" h.; cordial, 3.5" h.; cocktail, 5" h.; finger bowl, 4.5" dia. $20-25 ea.

Stem 526, goblet, moss green stem and crystal foot, 5.25" h. $12-15.

Stem 520, pair of cordials, Ingrid pattern, 3.125" h. $15-20 ea.

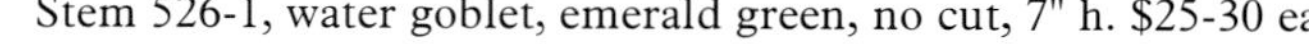

Stem 526-1, water goblet, emerald green, no cut, 7" h. $25-30 ea.

Left:
Stem 520, cordial, cut 520-4, 3.25" h. $25-30.

Stem 532, cut 1347 Woodcliff pattern: champagne, 4.25" h.; cocktail, 4" h.; juice, 5" h.; wine, 5" h.; cordial, 4.75" h. $15-20 ea.

Stem 553, water goblet, cut 553-1, 6" h. $15-20.

Stem 533, iced tea, cut 432-1/2, 7.25" h. $20-25.

Stem 553, cocktail, cut 1365 Fantasia pattern, 4" h. $10-15.

Stem 578, wine, cut 1379, 4.75" h. $15-20.

Stem 857, water goblet, cut 1341 Symphony pattern, 6.75" h. $10-15.

Stem 600, cordial, 3.5" h., and brandy, 3.75" h. $10-15 ea.

Stem 903, cocktails, Naomi pattern, cobalt bowl, with platinum encrusted decoration, and square foot, 4" h. $40-50.

Stem 903, cocktails, amber bowl, and square foot, 3.75" h. $18-20.

Stem 903, water goblet, ruby red, no cut, 5.5" h. $25-30.

Stem 903, wines, forest green bowl, and square foot, 4.375" h. $20-25.

Stem 903, water goblet, cut 121 Laurel pattern, 6" h. $20-25.

Stem 903, cordial, with square foot, cut 121 Laurel pattern, 4.75" h. $15-20.

Stem 903, champagne, cut 338 Canterbury pattern, 4.5" h. $20-25.

Stem 903, water goblet, cut 228, 6" h. $25-30.

Stem 905, water goblet, cut 121, 6" h. $15-20.

Stem 905, low wine, cut 338, 3.25" h. $15-20.

Stem 905, water goblet, cut 905-3, 6" h. $25-30.

Stem 905, water goblet, cut 480, 6" h. $20-25.

Stem 905, water goblet, cut 1211, 6" h. $10-15.

Stem 905-1/2, water goblet, in ritz blue, 5" h. $10-15.

Stem 907, water goblet, cut 907-1, 6.75" h. $10-15.

Trio of stem 909, cut 859 Prince of Wales pattern, with cut square foot: water goblet, 6" h.; champagne, 5" h.; cordial, 3.5" h. $20-25 ea.

Stem 909, cut 962-1/2: water goblet, 5.5" h.; champagne, 4.75" h.; cocktail, 4.5" h.; cordial, 3.25" h.; juice, 4.75" h.; claret, 4.25" h.; red wine, 4.625" h.; white wine, 4.25" h. $15-20 ea.

Stem 909 (square base), cut 962-1/2: water goblet, 6" h.; champagne, 4.5" h.; wine, 4.5" h.; cocktail, 4.5" h.; cordial, 3.125" h.; tumbler, 5" h. $15-20 ea.

Stem 912, cut 121 Laurel pattern and 39: water goblet, 6.625" h.; champagne, 5" h.; parfait, 6" h.; cocktail, 4.5" h.; low cocktail, 3" h.; wine, 4.5" h.; cordial, 3.75" h. $15-20 ea.

Stem 912, grouping of stemware, cut 121 Laurel pattern and cut 39: 6.25" h., 5" h., 4.5" h. $15-25 ea.

Stem 912, champagne, cut 121 Laurel pattern and cut 39, 4.5" h. $15-20.

Stem 912, wine, cut 121 Laurel pattern cut and 39, 4.5" h. $20-25.

Stem 912, water goblet, cut 121 Laurel pattern and cut 39, 6" h.; stem 914, iced tea, cut 121, 7" h. $15-20 ea.

Stem 914, cut 1012: iced tea, 6.25" h.; water goblet, 5.25" h.; juice, 5" h.; cocktail, 4.25" h.; red wine, 4.75" h.; white wine, 4.5" h.; brandy, 4.75" h.; low cocktail, 4.625" h., finger bowl, 4.5" dia. $20-25 ea.

Stem 914, water goblet, cut 1015, 6.25" h. $25-30.

Stem 915, cut 915-1: sherry, 5" h. $55-65; champagne, 5.5" h. $55-65; claret, 5" h. $55-65.
Stem 1939, cut 1939-2: wine, 5" h. $55-65; champagne, 7" h. $80-90.

Stem 915, cut 918-1/2 Empire pattern: water goblet, 7" h. $20-25; iced tea, 6.75" h. $20-25; champagne, 5.5" h. $20-25; saucer champagne, 4.5" h. $20-25; parfait, 7" h. $20-25; wine, 5.75" h. $20-25; juice, 4.875" h. $20-25; sherbet, 4.75" h. $20-25; wine, 5.5" h. $20-25; cocktail, 4" h. $20-25; roly poly, 2" h. $30-40.

Stem 916, cut 916-1: iced tea, 7" h. $50-60; champagne, 5.25" h. $50-60; parfait, 7" h. $50-60; wine, 5.25" h. $50-60; hollow stem wine, 5.25" h. $50-60; tumbler, 3.75" h. $25-30

Stem 916, hollow stem wine, cut 870, 5.5" h. $65-75.

Detail of hollow stem wine.

Trio of stem 916, cut 916-2: water goblet, 7" h. $70-80; wine, 5.5" h. $50-60; cocktail, 4.625" h. $50-60.

Stem 918, water goblet, no cut, with two bubbles in the stem, 7" h. $30-35.

Grouping of stem 918, cut 876, with blown bubble and stem, cut foot: water goblet, 7" h. $90-100; champagne, 5.5" h. $65-75; sherbet, 5" h. $65-75; wine, 5.75" h. $65-75.

Stem 918, water goblet, cut 933 Drury Lane pattern, 7" h. Note bubble in stem. $30-35.

Stem 918, cut 972: goblet, 7" h. $50-65; champagne, 5.5" h. $40-50.

Left:
Stem 925, water goblet, cut 925-2, 8" h. $20-25.

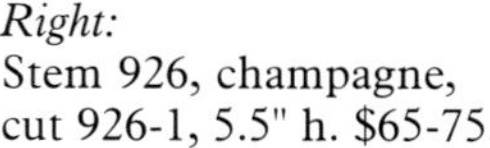

Right:
Stem 926, champagne, cut 926-1, 5.5" h. $65-75.

Stem 926, water goblet, cut 1075, 6.5" h. $65-75.

Grouping of stem 926, cut 1130, with bubble, cut foot: water goblet, 6.5" h. $70-80; champagne, 5.5" h. $60-70; cocktail, 3.25" h. $60-70; wine, 5" h. $60-70; finger bowl, 4.25" h. $35-40.

Stem 959, cordial, cut 39, 3.75" h. Stem 1282, cordial, cut 660, 4.5" h. $20-25 ea.

Stem 959, water goblet, cut 859, 7.5" h. $15-20.

Stem 960, cut 1434 Heirloom pattern: water goblet, 7" h., and iced tea, 6.25" h. $15-20 ea.

Stem 963, cordial, cut 1158. 4" h. $25-30.

Stem 960, water goblet, cut 1435 Old Master patttern, 7" h. $25-30.

Stem 966, champagne, cut 1032, 5" h. $45-55.

Stem 970, wine, cut 43, signed "Tiffany" on bottom, 5.25" h. $25-30.

Stem 970, wine (frosted), cut 900, 7.25" h. $20-25.

Stem 970, water goblet, cut 1446 Wicker pattern, 8.5" h. $25-35.

Stem 970, wine, cut 1447 Sunburst pattern, 7.25" h. $20-25.

Stem 971, brandy, cut 774, 5" h. $15-20.

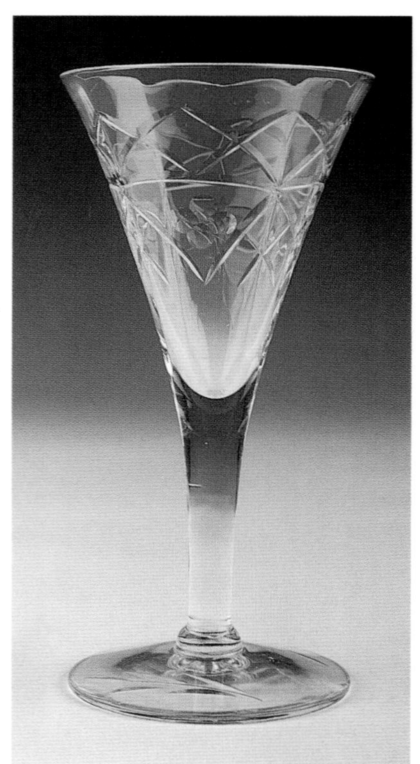

Stem 971, brandy, cut 832, 4.75" h. $10-15.

Stem 972, champagne, cut 1463 Coronet pattern, 6" h. $20-25.

Stem 981, water goblet (frosted), cut 1452 Rosalynn pattern, 7" h. $40-50.

Stem 981, water goblet (frosted), cut 1453 Majestic pattern, 7" h. $30-40.

Stem 981, water goblet, cut 1453 Majestic pattern, 7.75" h. $45-55.

Stem 981, wine, cut 1453 Majestic pattern, 6.75" h. $30-35.

Stem 981, cut 1453 Majestic pattern: champagne, 5.425" h.; water goblet, 7.75" h.; wine, 6.625" h. $50-60.

Stem 982, two water goblets, cut 1454 Grand Baroque pattern, a.k.a. "Baroque," 7.5" h. $45-55 ea.

Stem 982, wine, cut 1454 Grand Baroque pattern, a.k.a. "Baroque," 6.25" h. $50-60.

Stem 982, cut 1455 Dorchester pattern: water goblet, 7.5" h.; wine, 6.375" h.; sherbet, 5.5" h. $35-40 ea.

Stem 982, water goblet, cut 1455
Dorchester pattern, 7.5" h. $45-55.

Detail of cutwork.

Stem 993, cut 1012 Adams pattern: iced tea, 6.5" h. $15-20; water goblet, 7.25" h. $20-25; champagne, 6" h. $15-20.

Stem 982, cordial, cut 1455
Dorchester pattern, 4.875" h. $45-55.

Stem 1030, Dutch brandy, cut 859, 6.25" h. $55-65.

Stem 1030, Dutch brandy, cut 1451 Brittany pattern, 6.25" h. $55-65.

Detail of reeded stem.

Stem 1208, brandy snifter, cut 967, 5" h. $20-25.

Stem 1217, brandy snifter, cut 220 Pineapple pattern, 5" h. $30-35.

Stem 1235, water goblet, cut 1419 Solitaire pattern, 7" h. $15-20.

Stem 1282 (twisted), water goblet, no cut, Astrid pattern in pink, 6.75" h. $20-25.

Stem 1217, water goblet, cut 738, 7.25" h. $25-30.

Stem 1282 (twisted), water goblet, no cut, Astrid pattern, 7" h. $10-15.

Stem 1282, water goblet, cut 659, 6.75" h. $20-25.

Stem 1282, water goblet, cut 660, 6.75" h. $25-30.

Stem 1350, water goblet, cut 1350-5, 6.5" h. $10-15.

Right:
Stem 1476, water goblet, cut 627, 8" h. $15-20.

Stem 1350, water goblet, cut 1350-3, 6.75" h. $10-15.

Stem 1350, water goblet, cut 1350-7, 6.5" h. $10-15.

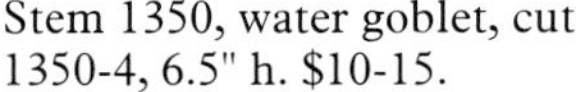

Stem 1350, water goblet, cut 1350-4, 6.5" h. $10-15.

Right:
Stem 1479, water goblet, cut 94, 6.625" h. $15-20.

Stem 1479, water goblet, cut 808, 7" h. $20-25.

Stem 1482, cut 583: goblet, 8.5" h. $50-65; champagne, 6.25" h. $40-50; wine, 5.5" h. $40-50.

Below:
Stem 1479, cut 858: water goblet, 7" h. $15-20; iced tea, 6.75" h. $15-20; champagne, 5.5" h. $15-20; sherbet, 4.5" h. $15-20; cordial, 4.5" h. $15-20; cocktail, 4" h. $15-20; low wine, 4" h. $15-20; claret, 5.5" h. $15-20; sherry, 6" h. $15-20; white wine, 5.75" h. $15-20; red wine, 6" h. $15-20; bottle, no. 2, half pint, 6.5" h. $25-30.

Stem 1934, champagne, cut 1934-1, 6.5" h. $70-80.

Stem 1936, water goblet, cut 1936-1, 8" h. $75-85.

Stem 1936, hollow stem wine, cut 800, 5.25" h. $85-100.

Stem 1936, brandy, cut 1936-1, 5.875" h. $80-90.

Stem 1937 (air blown twist stem), wine, no cut, 7" h. $150-175.

Stem 1939, water goblet, cut 1939-2, 6.75" h. $80-90.

Stem 1941, water goblet, cut 1204, 7.5" h. $25-30.

Stem 1962, water goblet, no cut, Chantilly gold band pattern, 6.5" h. $10-15.

Stem 1951, water goblet, cut 1951-1, 6.75" h. $15-20.

Stem 1962, water goblet, cut 1447, 6.5" h. $15-20.

Stem 1964, cut 1424 Empress pattern: iced tea, 6.25" h.; water goblet, 6.25" h.; wine, 5.5" h.; claret, 4.5" h.; cordial, 3.75" h.; cocktail, 4.25" h. $10-15 ea.

Stem 1965, water goblet, cut 1418 Tuxedo pattern, 6.75" h. $10-15.

Stem 1965, water goblet, cut 1421 Anniversary pattern, 7.25" h. $20-25.

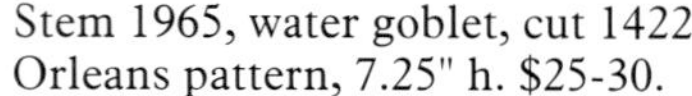

Stem 1965, water goblet, cut 1422 Orleans pattern, 7.25" h. $25-30.

Stem 1965, water goblet, cut 1965-1, 7.25" h. $20-25.

Stem 1966, water goblet, cut 1966-3, 7" h. $10-15.

Stem 1967, water goblet, cut 1967-2, 6.75" h. $10-15.

Stem 1966, water goblet, cut 1439 Bridal Tiara pattern, 7" h. $15-20.

Stem 1967, water goblet, cut 1967-1, 6.75" h. $15-20.

Stem 1971, water goblet, with gold trim, cut 1971-1, 7" h. $15-20.

Stem 1971, gold trim water goblet, 5.75" h.; brandy or cordial, 3.875" h. $15-20 ea.

Stem 1977, sherry, cut 43 Falerno pattern, 6" h. $15-20.

Stem 1978, red wines, cut 43, "Ultra" shape, 7.5" h. $15-20.

Stem 1973, sherbet or cocktail, in pink, with crystal foot, cut 1443 Enchantment pattern, 11 oz., 4.875" h. NP.

Stem 1978, water goblet, unidentified cut, 8.75" h. $15-20.

Stem 2000, water goblet, cut 941, 7" h. $55-65.

Stem 2503, water goblet, cut 713, 5.5" h. $25-30.

Stem 2812, water goblet, cut 1076, 6.75" h. $35-40.

Stem 3050, goblet, cut 936, 4.75" h. $20-25.

Stem 2690, water goblet, emerald green, unfinished, no cut, 5.25" h. $15-20.

Stem 3050, water goblet, ruby red, no cut, 5.5" h. $25-30.

Stem 3214, water goblet, unidentified cut, 5.75" h. *Courtesy of Steve and Anna Britvec.* $15-20.

Stem 3600, water goblet, etched pattern candlewick with ruby red foot, 4.25" h. $25-30.

Stem 3214, water goblet, gold band, 6" h. $12-15.

Stem 3600, cocktail, etched pattern candlewick, 4" h. $20-25.

Stem 4805, cut 907: water goblet, 8.5" h. $100-110; champagne, 7" h. $65-75; cordial, 5" h. $100-110; hollow stem wine, 8" h. $65-75; red wine, 7" h. $65-75; sherry, 6" h. $65-75.

Stem 4805, cut 4805-1 Tapestry pattern, with jeweled stem and cut foot: water goblet, 8.5" h. $90-100; tall champagne, 7.25" h. $30-40; sherbet or low champagne, 6" h. $30-40; white wine, 7" h. $30-40; sherry, 6" h. $30-40; port wine, 5.75" h. $30-40; finger bowl, 2.25" h., 4" dia. $65-75.

Stem 4816, water goblet, cut 1401, 8.125" h. $25-30.

Stem 4816, water goblet, cut 1401, 8.25" h. This stem cut differs from the usual stem line 4816. $20-25.

Stem 4816, claret, cut 1401, 6.625" h. $25-30.

Stem 4816, champagne, cut 4816-2, 7" h. $45-55.

Detail to show cut of foot.

Stem 5108, cordial, unidentified cut, 4" h. $20-25.

Stem 5584, water goblet, cut 1063, 8" h. $25-30.

Stem 9936, water goblet, cut 739, 7.5" h. $25-30.

Stem 9936, water goblet, cut 991, 7.5" h. $20-25.

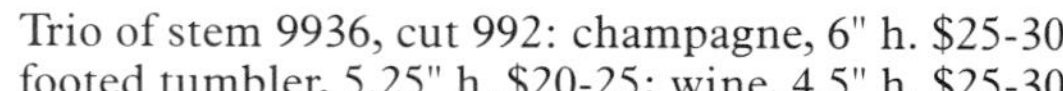

Trio of stem 9936, cut 992: champagne, 6" h. $25-30; footed tumbler, 5.25" h. $20-25; wine, 4.5" h. $25-30.

Stem 9079, wine, frosted square foot, 4" h. $15-20.

Stem 9936, water goblet, cut 9936-3, 7.5" h. $50-60.

Stem 9936, water goblet, cut 9936-4, 7.75" h. $25-30.

Stem 10007, water goblet, unidentified cut, 7.25" h. (This stem number designation was assigned in the book by Page et al. 1995 and not by the Seneca Glass Company). $80-90.

Stem 10012, water goblet, cut 10012-1, 5.75" h. (This stem number designation was assigned in the book by Page et al. 1995 and not by the Seneca Glass Company). $30-35.

~Sugar Bowls & Creamer~

Open handled sugar, unidentified cut, 3.5" h. $70-80.

Individual creamer, 2.25" h. $45-55.

Open handled sugar, rose cut, 3.5" h. $70-80.

~Tumblers~

Whiskey, 2.25" h. NP.

Whiskey, unidentified cut, 2.5" h. $10-15.

Whiskey, unidentified cut, 2.25" h. $15-20.

Old Fashion, no cut, monogrammed "C" and pilgrim hat design, 3.875" h. $15-20.

Neptune pattern, footed tumbler, 3.75" h. $15-20.

Tumbler, unidentified cut, 4.25" h. $20-25.

Detail of label.

Old Fashion, with etching and cut 39, 3.5" h. $15-20.

Tumbler, cut 45, 10 oz., 4.75" h. NP.

Left:
Tumbler, deep etch 448, 3.75" h. $25-30.

Tumbler, cut 647, 5.5" h. $18-20.

Whiskey, cut 121 Laurel pattern and cut 39, 2.5" h. $15-20.

Tumbler, cut 460 and 43, 2.75" h. $25-30.

Whiskey, cut 1448 Chalice pattern, 2.75" h. $15-20.

Whiskey, cut 144, 3 oz., 2.25" h. $15-20.

Left:
Tumbler, deep etch 608, 3.5" h. $15-20.

Tumbler, cut 1451 Brittany pattern, 5" h. $20-25.

Tumbler, cut 1453 Majestic pattern, 5" h. $35-40.

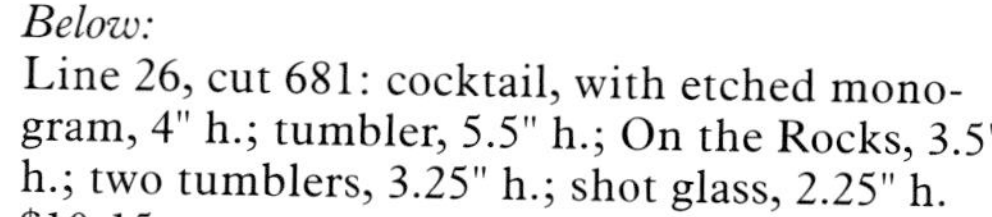

Below:
Line 26, cut 681: cocktail, with etched monogram, 4" h.; tumbler, 5.5" h.; On the Rocks, 3.5" h.; two tumblers, 3.25" h.; shot glass, 2.25" h. $10-15 ea.

On the Rocks, cut 1452 Rosalynn pattern, 4.25" h. $35-40.

Detail of cocktail, with etched monogram.

Line 85, cut 837: iced tea, 7" h.; cocktail, 3.5" h.; footed juice/tumbler, 3.5" h.; tumbler, 4.25" h. $15-20.

Line 100-R, tumblers, in burgundy, 12 oz., 10 oz., 5 oz., and 2 oz. $12-15 ea.

Line 105, whiskeys, in forest green and apple green, 2 oz. $10-15 ea.

Line 101, tumblers, in burgundy, 3.5" h. and 5" h. $10-15 ea.

Line 190, cut 720: tumblers, 3.75" to 5.375" h. $18-25. Footed, 5.25" h. $18-25. Cocktail, 5.25" h. $15-20.

Line 260, cut 774: tumblers, footed, 3.25" to 6.25" h.; On the Rocks, 3.25" h. (and finger bowl, 4.5" h.). $15-20 ea.

Line 260, tumblers, cut 774, 3.75" to 5.5" h. $15-20 ea.

Line 285, tumbler, cut 646, 5.5" h. $10-15.

Line 476, tumbler, cut 1074 Spray pattern, 5.5" h. $15-20.

Line 909, On the Rocks, with cut square bottom, cut 859 Prince of Wales pattern, 4.5" h. $15-20

Line 388, iced tea, cut 1111, 7" h. $15-20.

Line 492, tumblers, footed, cut 692, 3.5" to 5" h. (and cocktail, unidentified stem, cut 692, 3.5" h.). $20-25 ea.

Right:
Line 908, tumbler, cut 859, 4.25" h. $10-15.

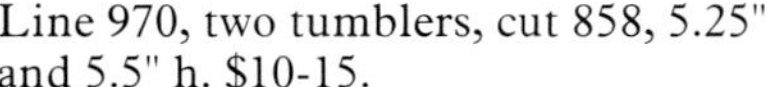

Line 970, two tumblers, cut 858, 5.25" and 5.5" h. $10-15.

Line 972, cut 1449 Tapestry pattern: On the Rocks, 3.5" h., and hi-ball, 4.5" h. $35-40 ea.

Line 972, cut 1449 Tapestry pattern: Old Fashion, 3.5" h., and two On the Rocks, 4.375" h. $25-35 ea.

Line 1553, tumblers, in smoke, 3.5" h. and 4.5" h. $5-10 ea.

Line 1939, tumbler, cut 777, 5.5" h. $35-40

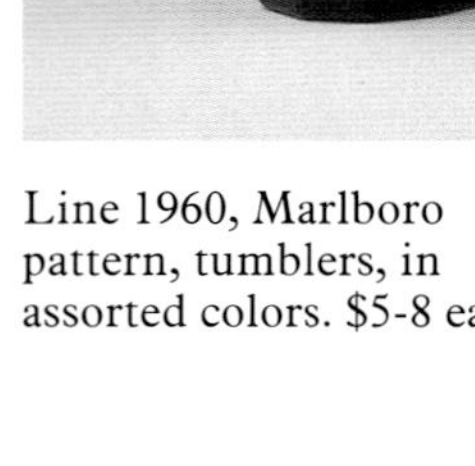

Line 1960, Marlboro pattern, tumblers, in assorted colors. $5-8 ea.

Line 3800, tumblers, decoration 405, in gold, and decoration 491, in blue and gold, 14 oz., 6" h. $10-15 ea.

Below:
Line 1960, Marlboro pattern, eight tumblers, in assorted colors, 4.5" h. (in metal carrier or holder). $55-65 set.

Line 18401, tumblers, decoration 488, gold rims, 5 oz. and 12 oz. $10-15 ea.

Line 3800, tumbler, decoration 484, in red and gold, 11 oz., 4" h. $10-15.

Line 3800, Old Fashion, peacock optic, 11 oz., 3.75" h. $5-10.

~Tumble Ups~

Tumble up, cut 12 Laurel pattern, 6.5" h. (overall), glass: 3" h. $35-45.

~Vases~

Vase, footed, unidentified cut, 10.5" h. $80-100.

Below:
Rolled edge vase, unidentified cut, 3.5" h., 7.25" dia. $110-120.

Vase, footed, unidentified cut, 18" h. (available in three different sizes). $1800.

Vase, in accent red, 4.125" h. $15-20.

Vase and tumbler, cut 360, 5.25" h. and 3.75" h. $20-25; $15-20.

Vase, in cobalt, 8" h. $45-55.

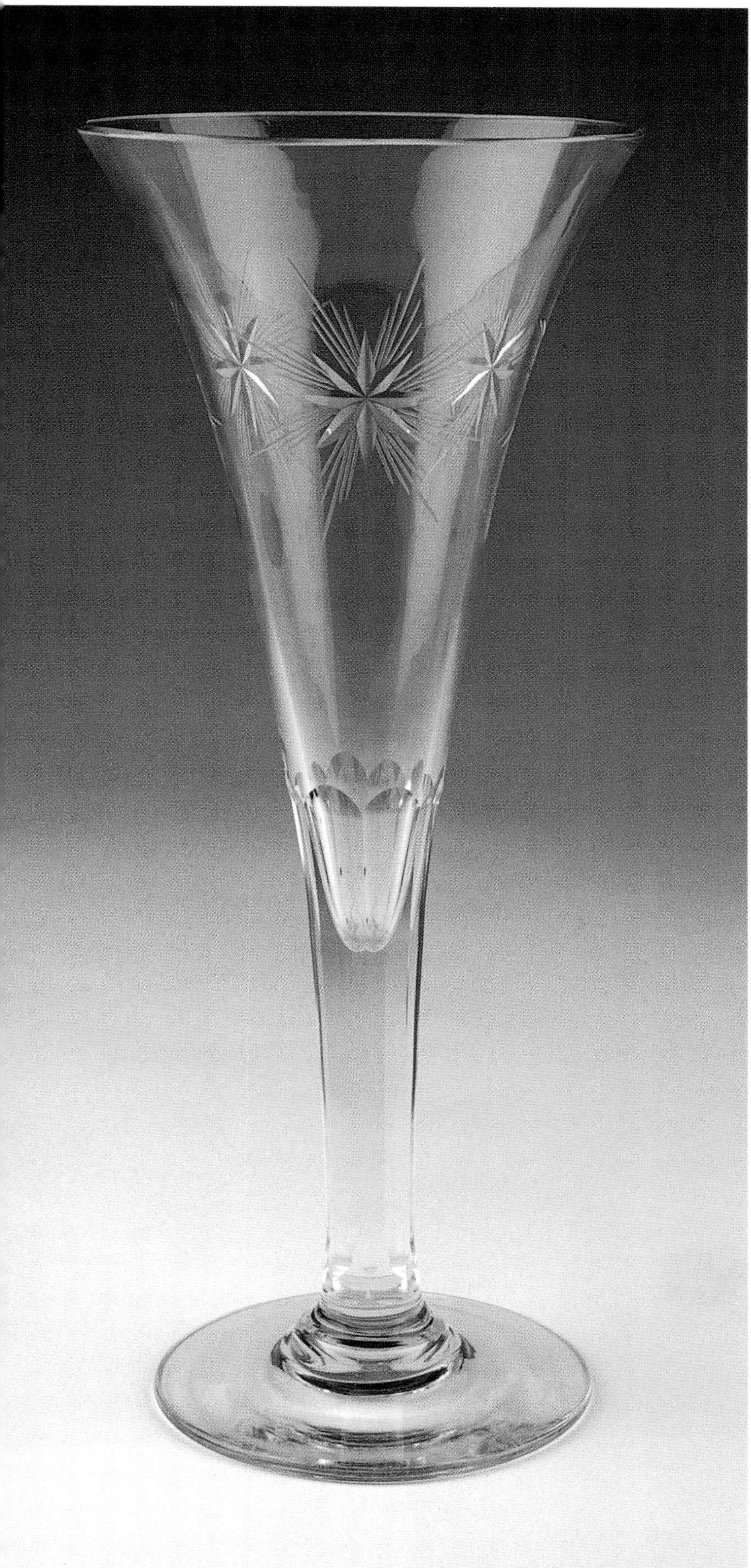

Stem 43, trumpet vase, cut 360, 12" h. $110-125.

45-8 vase, black foot, 10" h.
$40-50.

Bibliography

Aull, William J., Jr. *Sand, fire n' things. Beaumont Company, Davis-Lynch Glass Co., Morgantown Glassware Guild, Seneca Glass Company.* Produced in cooperation with the four companies listed, c. 1965.

Bureau of Industrial Hygiene. *A Report on the Glass Industry in West Virginia.* West Virginia: State Health Department (study conducted in the winter of 1937-38).

China, Glass, and Lamps. "New Wares For 1934 Featured Successful Exhibitions For Trade. Advance in Dinnerware Design and Decoration Received Wide Attention. Attendance and Business in Pittsburgh Well Ahead of 1933. Return of Liquors Helped Glass." 1934.

Comstock, Jim (ed). *The West Virginia Heritage Encyclopedia.* Volumes 10 & 11. Richwood, West Virginia: Jim Comstock, 1974.

Comstock, Jim (ed). *The West Virginia Heritage Encyclopedia.* Volume 20. Richwood, West Virginia: Jim Comstock, 1976.

Core, Earl L. *The Monongalia Story. A Bicentennial History.* Parsons, West Virginia: McClain Printing Company, 1982.

Core, Earl L. *The Monongalia Story. A Bicentennial History.* Parsons, West Virginia: McClain Printing Company, 1984.

Fleming Associates, Delores A. "Seneca Glass Company. 1891-1983." Pamphlet prepared by Delores A. Fleming Associates, History Contractors, 1986.

Julian, Norman. "'The First Century is the Hardest.' A Morgantown Centenarian Reminisces On Glassmaking and Poetry Writing." *Goldenseal* 6 (1), January-March 1980.

Manning, Martha. "West Virginia Cut Crystal." *Goldenseal. West Virginia Traditional Life* 10 (1), Spring 1984.

McKenzie, L. E. *Morgantown District Industrial and Business Survey.* Morgantown, West Virginia: Morgantown Chamber of Commerce, 1921.

Page, Bob and Dale Frederiksen. *Seneca Glass Company. 1891-1983. A Stemware Identification Guide.* Greensboro, North Carolina: Page-Frederiksen Publishing Company, 1995.

Phillips, Phoebe (ed.). *The Encyclopedia of Glass.* New Yor Crown Publishers, Inc., 1981.

Piña, Leslie. *Popular '50s and '60s Glass. Color Along t River.* Atglen, Pennsylvania: Schiffer Publishing Lt 1995.

Robinson, Felix G. "Seneca in its Sixty Seventh Yea *Tableland Trails* II (I), Spring 1955.

Seneca Glass Company. *History of Seneca Glass Compan Beechurst Avenue between 6th and 8th Stree Morgantown, West Virginia. "American Craftsmanship its Best ... since 1891."* Company produced materi 1963.

Six, Dean. "Decorating Techniques at Seneca Glass." *Gl Collector's Digest* IV (6), April/May 1991.

Snyder, Jeffrey B. *Morgantown Glass: From Depression Gl Through the 1960s.* Atglen, Pennsylvania: Schiffer Pu lishing Ltd., 1998.

United States Tariff Commission. *Household Glasswa Former Workers of the Morgantown Glassware Guild In Morgantown, West Virginia.* Washington, D.C.: T Publications 456, 1972.

Warrin, Edmondson. "And Now—A Toast! May Repe Bring Fine Glassware Once More Into Its Own *Crockery and Glass Journal*, October 1933.

Weatherman, Hazel Marie. *Colored Glassware of the D pression Era 2.* Ozark, Missouri: A Glassbooks Produ tion, 1974.

Weiner, Robert Stanley. *The Location and Distribution the Glass Industry of Ohio, Pennsylvania, and West V ginia.* Pittsburgh, Pennsylvania: University of Pitt burgh, 1949.

Wiley, James A. "Morgantown's Decorated Glass." *Topi Old Morgantown Glass Collectors' Guild, Inc.* 7 (3), Su mer 1996.

Zembala, Dennis Michael. *Machines in the Glasshouse: T Transformation of Work in the Glass Industry. 1820-191* Ph.D. Dissertation for The George Washington Ur versity, September 30, 1984.

Index